OZ AND JAMES'S BIG WINE ADVENTURE

Paris

CHAMPAGNE

Reims

R. Marne

Epernay

Chouilly

Strasbourg

ALSACE

R. RHIN

Mulhouse

LOIRE VALLEY

R. Loir

R. Loire

Angers

Tours

Nantes

VIN

BORDEAUX

BERGERAC

ATLANTIC
OCEAN

Bordeaux

Bergerac

R. Garonne

Monbazillac

R. Dordogne

Arcachon

Bazas

SOUTH WEST

CAHORS

Cahors

BUZET

Gaillac

JURANÇON

MADIRAN

GAILLAC

R. Aude

ROSÉ

LANGUEDOC
-ROUSSILLON

BURGUNDY

Dijon

Beaune

Mâcon

BEAUJOLAIS

Villefranche
-sur-saône

R. Saône

Lyon

Orange

Avignon

JURA

L'Etoile

R. Rhône

SAVOIE

RHÔNE
VALLEY

Die

PROVENCE

Nice

St. Tropez

Nîmes

Marseille

Sète

MEDITERRANEAN
SEA

CORSICA

Bastia

Ajaccio

OZ AND JAMES'S
BIG WINE ADVENTURE

OZ CLARKE AND JAMES MAY

with Julie Arkell

1 3 5 7 9 10 8 6 4 2

Published in 2006 by BBC Books, an imprint of Ebury Publishing

Ebury Publishing is a division of the Random House Group

The Random House Group Limited Reg. No. 954009

Addresses for companies within the Random House Group can be found at
www.randomhouse.co.uk

A CIP catalogue record for this book is available from the British Library

The Random House Group Limited makes every effort to ensure that the papers used in our
books are made from trees that have been legally sourced from well-managed and credibly
certified forests. Our paper procurement policy can be found on www.randomhouse.co.uk

Commissioning editor: Stuart Cooper
Project editor: Eleanor Maxfield
Copy editor: Helen Armitage
Designer: Smith & Gilmour
Production controller: Kenneth McKay

Designed and typeset by Smith & Gilmour, London
Printed and bound in Great Britain by CPI Bath

ISBN 0 563 53900 3
ISBN (from Jan 2007) 978 0 563 53900 1

CONTENTS

INTRODUCTION ABOUT THIS BOOK

OK, so you love French wines already and want
to learn more about them. Or perhaps you're a
beer drinker who's watched the TV series this
book accompanies and been inspired to undergo
a conversion. Either way, the book will not
disappoint you. Inside these pages is a wealth of
region-by-region information that will increase
your understanding of French wines – and that will
enhance your enjoyment of drinking them. It will
guide you to making better choices when you order
French wine in a restaurant and when you buy it
in a shop (or even at a French winery).

In addition, you'll find all sorts of practical hints and tips for planning
your own big wine adventure – for example, the best ways of getting to
France, what local food specialities you should try when you're there
(not to forget which French wines can be drunk with what when you're
back home) and how to look after the wines you've ferried (or tunnelled)
across the English Channel – or should that be La Manche?! At the back
of the book there are the names of the best companies offering organized
wine holidays in France; if you're going DIY, you'll also find the addresses
of all the major tourist offices that can help point the way to a good tour
of the various producers that welcome visitors.

The book follows the route that was taken in the TV series across the wine regions of France. Not every nook and cranny could be visited, of course, but fear not! The best of the missing bits are included here, which will prove useful when you are planning your stay in France. Having said that, this book is not an attempt to be the definitive, all-singing, all-dancing, exhaustive guide to French wines – which is why you will find pointers to more specialist books in the Appendix (see page 220).

The world of French wine

There's always a ding-dong battle with Italy, but in most years France usually wins the honour of being the world's largest producer of wine. But is France the producer of the best wine in the world? That is an altogether very different question. Well, the answer to this is yes and no. 'Yes' because many French wines, most especially the top-flight reds and whites from the regions of Bordeaux, Burgundy and the Rhône valley, simply cannot be emulated by any other winemaking country, as hard as anyone tries (and try they do). The point here is that there's no doubt that France has created the model for the rest of the winemaking world. So where does the 'no' bit come in? Well, put simply, at the bottom end of the quality wine scale, France is as guilty as any other winemaking country of producing its fair share of utter dross, wines that verge on the undrinkable. But after you've read this book, you won't be drinking any more of these, will you?

A fine example of France's far-reaching global influence is its classic grape varieties, which have been grown in French soil for over 2000 years (Provence is the country's oldest winemaking region). Many are the originals of the varieties that have now become international superstars: Cabernet Sauvignon, Merlot, Chardonnay and Pinot Noir (to name but a few). This wouldn't have happened without France acting as the pathfinder, lighting the way to show the world where these grapes like to grow and how they should be turned into good wine.

French winemakers have also always held dear the concept of 'terroir', a concept that embraces the belief that every vineyard has its own unique 'address' in terms of its relationship to soil, climate, topography and exposure to the sun, which dictates the grape variety that should be grown where. This concept is now being taken more seriously by New World countries (Australia, New Zealand, South Africa, South America and the USA), which often used to dismiss terroir out of hand.

Interestingly, while the New World has striven to imitate France's benchmark wines, in turn many of their best practices are now trickling into France. In consequence, many French wines are much better made and are much easier to drink than they once were, even in the most traditional of regions, such as Bordeaux and Burgundy.

It has been the character and quality of French wines that have proved the hallmarks of their success and a mere glance at any schoolboy geography book gives all the clues as to why. Lying between the 40th and 50th parallels north, the latitude of France is ideal for wine production, offering everything from the chilly, windy and wet climate of the north of the country to the blistering, bone-dry heat of the south. There's also tremendous geographical diversity in terms of the variety of different soil types so that every major (and a host of minor) grape varieties can make a good home here. Furthermore, French winemaking knowledge has been passed down from generation to generation since medieval times, giving almost insuperable expertise. All this means that France is able to produce wine of every style and flavour to match every taste at a range of prices to suit every pocket. It gives us everything, from the traditional classics of Bordeaux and Burgundy that have seemingly been made for ever to the new-wave, New World-style wonders emerging from parts of the south. And there is plenty of it (too much, in fact). A fairly unbeatable formula for success you would think ... but read on.

Some statistics ... and a warning

More red and rosé wines (64 per cent, to be precise) are made than white, the majority hailing from the southern half of the country – it must be remembered that northern France is at the climatic limits of grape-growing and red grapes struggle to ripen properly here.

On average, France produces around 19 per cent of all the world's wine, a whopping 52 million hl of wine each year (that's 1,143,870,000 gal. in old money). Some 55 per cent of this is of appellation-contrôlée status (wine made under the strictest of rules – see page 18) and 31 per cent is Vins de Pays (country wine). Doing the sums, therefore, that leaves 7,280,000 hl (160,141,800 gal.) of plonk. The vineyards cover a total of 860,000 ha (2,124,200 acres) shared among 145,000 grape growers.

There is a storm brewing on the horizon, however. The European Union has drawn up radical proposals to tackle the crisis of wine over-production across Europe (about 300 million litres/66 million gal. of wine from France and Italy alone is being turned into ethanol or surgical spirit in 2006 – a policy called 'crisis distillation'). Its blueprint calls for more than 10 per cent of Europe's vineyards to be pulled up by 2011 – and growers will be paid to do so. This isn't the first time this has happened in France, though. In the 1980s, over 30,000 ha (74,000 acres) of vines were uprooted in the Languedoc-Roussillon region in an effort to curb over-production of sub-standard wine.

Digging up vineyards will not solve the problem alone, however. Apart from the knock-on effect of falling domestic consumption, France is losing sales in the UK, one of its vital export markets, to the wines of the New World (to Australia and California in particular). The country has wasted valuable time by not addressing this problem before now, although the French government has now pledged a 40 per cent increase in funds to tackle the marketing of French wines in the UK. So how could things change? Well, for example, winemaking laws could be relaxed to allow the use of oak chips to simulate barrel ageing, a technique that is used widely in the production of New World wines. Perhaps most importantly – as the relative success of the Vins de Pays has shown –

simpler labelling and greater use of brand names would be popular
with UK consumers. Vins de Pays usually state on the label the name
of the grape variety from which they have been made, whereas the
vast majority of appellation contrôlée wines are named after the place
where the grapes were grown and, furthermore, are often subject to
complicated, hierarchical wine-classification systems that can be
difficult to get to grips with. Vin de Pays Syrah can now even be labelled
Vin de Pays Shiraz in recognition of the fact that UK drinkers are very
familiar with this name, thanks to Australian versions (Syrah and Shiraz
are exactly the same grape variety). This tiny change alone will allow
producers to compete head-on with their New World peers. France
needs more initiatives like this if it is to win back its place in our hearts
and on our tables – and before we forget the thrilling flavours that
it offers.

In the vineyard

'Great wine is made from great grapes.' This is the mantra of all producers of quality wine, who recognize that it is impossible to craft good wine from bad grapes. So how do they achieve this?

When a wine producer chooses a new vineyard site, he or she will take into consideration its altitude, topography, aspect, climate, soil and the availability of water. Much thought will go into selecting the grape variety that will best match all of these criteria. How close to one another the vines are planted, how the vines are trained and pruned, and when the grapes are harvested are equally important. If the vine is planted in the best possible place, it will provide top quality grapes and, in turn, top quality wine, though in France, many grape growers (especially those in the north of the country) have to keep all their fingers and toes crossed because the quality of their crop is largely in the hands of nature.

Matchmaking

Climate very much influences the choice of grape variety grown. The red Mourvèdre variety will not ripen unless it is planted in regions that boast roasting heat and long hours of sunshine and is therefore unsuitable for cool climates, whereas the white Riesling grape variety prefers cool conditions in which it can ripen slowly over a long period.

In general, all vines perform best in the kind of infertile, free-draining soils we wouldn't want in our back garden, where they must send their roots deep into the ground in their scrabble for nutrients and water. Having said that, though, some soils suit certain grape varieties better than others. Chardonnay, for example, performs best when planted in limestone soils, while gravel favours Cabernet Sauvignon.

In France, centuries of trial and error have determined which grape variety grows best where, but this doesn't mean that the era of experimentation is over, as the south of the country is proving. Aimé Guibert at Mas de Daumas Gassac provides the perfect example of a producer who has planted a wide range of non-traditional grape varieties to stunning effect.

Canopy management

This ensures that the foliage is kept under control in order to balance shade and sunshine so that the grapes ripen to perfection. In the south of France, where it is very hot in summer, most grape varieties require a dense leaf canopy to protect them from sunburn, but in the cooler climate of northerly parts of the country, grapes will not ripen if the foliage provides too much shade.

The acid test

The word 'acidity' may conjure up negative images of vats of sulphuric acid and other caustic chemicals, but natural fruit acids are essential for wine. As a rule, grapes grown in the north of France are more likely to produce wines with higher acidity levels because the grapes don't always ripen properly thanks to the cooler climate.

The timing of the grape harvest

If the grapes are picked too early, they will lack sugar and flavour; too late, and the over-ripe grapes will lack refreshing acidity and aroma. Grape growers therefore aim to produce perfectly ripened grapes that possess the perfect balance of natural sugars and just the right amount of natural acidity. Some styles, however, actively need grapes with low-sugar and high-acid levels – champagne provides the perfect model here because it needs to start off life as a very tart wine. In complete contrast, some sweet wines are made from ultra-ripe grapes that have been left, quite literally, to rot on the vine to give very concentrated and very sweet grape juice.

A year in the life of a vine

Spring As the weather starts to warm up and the days begin to lengthen, the vine's sap rises and the buds burst to reveal the vine's leaves. The biggest danger at this time is frost because it can destroy vulnerable young buds – no buds, no grapes, no wine! Pest and disease control are also critical at this time of year – the vine is often sprayed to protect it from potential problems (cool, wet areas where fungal diseases are rife require the most protection) – and the soil beneath it is cleared of weeds

13

**THE CONCEPT
OF 'TERROIR'**
There is no direct
translation of this French
word into English, but
in essence it means that
each vineyard has its own
unique 'address' that
reflects the interaction
of its soil, topography,
climate and exposure
to the sun. A sense of
place, in other words.

(the hoeing in itself helps to put some air into the soil). As the vine grows, new shoots are tied to the trellising wires; training systems are often determined by years of tradition and of knowing what system works best where.

Summer The vine flowers for about ten days, during which time pollinations and fertilization occurs. The flowers then set into clusters of what will become the fruit. Hot, dry weather is critical – rain or cold causes poor fruit set or disease and the size of the crop is therefore reduced. The vine needs water at this point, however, if fruit set is to be successful, so it plunges its roots deep into the earth in search of it (irrigation is not permitted in France). If the fruit needs more sunlight, leaf plucking (the removal of excess leaves) is carried out and when the grapes increase in size and change colour from green to translucent gold, dark red or black (called 'véraison') green harvesting (the removal of excess grape clusters) is done if the grower wishes to reduce crop levels to enhance the quality of the remaining grapes.

Autumn This is what everyone has worked so hard for – the harvest! In France, the grapes are usually picked in September or October. The last thing anyone needs right now is a downpour because this will cause the grapes to become bloated with water, diluting the flavours contained within their pulp.

Winter Time, now, for a much deserved rest – indeed, a period of dormancy is essential to the vine's health. It sheds its leaves, the sap descends and the vine goes to sleep. Snow, ice, frost and wind won't disturb it. The grower doesn't relax, though – this is a great time of year for pruning, which is by far the best way of controlling the yield of grapes for next year's harvest (the lower the yield, the better the wine).

The winemaking process

Wouldn't it be great if winemaking could be described as putting the fruit in at one end and drinking the liquid that comes out at the other? It's not quite as straightforward as this, of course, but the process can nevertheless be summed up neatly in six steps.

Sorting and de-stemming After the grapes have been picked, they are brought to the winery, where they are usually sorted to discard any fruit of poor quality. The stems and stalks are removed because they would otherwise impart a nasty, highly astringent taste to the wine.

Crushing The grapes are now crushed to break their skins so that the yeasts (either the native ones found naturally on the grape skins and in the atmosphere of the cellar, or the induced, laboratory-cultured strains that are more predictable) can get to work on the juice and fermentation can begin.

For white wines, the grapes are also pressed at this point so that all of their juice is squeezed out (though not too forcefully because nobody wants the bitter, woody flavours of squashed pips). The juice is then usually whisked away from the skins as quickly as possible – most whites don't benefit from prolonged skin contact (where the juice and the skins are allowed to mix together), thanks to the undesirable, mouth-puckering effect of tannin, a substance found naturally in grape skins. Some wines, such as Sauvignon Blanc, may have a few hours of skin contact, however, because Sauvignon skins contain a lovely leafy, nettley flavour that tastes great in the wine – and this needs to be extracted.

When it comes to red wines, the skins need to soak in the juice to coax out all the hidden perfumes and flavours contained within the skins and, of course, to leach out their colour (even red grapes have white pulp). Fortunately, the tannin extracted at the same time is advantageous here, by acting as a preservative and anti-oxidant.

Alcoholic fermentation Wine is fermented in stainless-steel, fibreglass or epoxy resin-lined concrete tanks, though oak barrels are often used for top wines. The yeasts convert the grape sugars into alcohol and carbon dioxide gas. Fermentation ceases when the yeasts die because

15

they have either used up all of the sugars, giving a dry wine, or they've been killed through alcohol poisoning, in which case there will still be some natural sweetness left in the juice.

White wines are fermented at lower temperatures than red wines (around 18°C (64°F) versus 32°C (90°F)) to preserve freshness, fruitiness, delicacy and aroma. For red wines, both the juice and skins are fermented together and the skins are pressed afterwards.

Malolactic fermentation Sorry for the long words. In effect, this is a secondary fermentation brought about by the action of bacteria that turn tart malic acid (think cooking apples) to the softer, rounder lactic acid (think milk). Because this phenomenon can occur spontaneously, the winemaker has to think ahead. Wines of very high natural acidity benefit from 'the malo', as winemakers call it, so if he or she wants to make sure that the wine is less aggressive, then the wine is injected with lactic bacteria. If, on the other hand, the winemaker desires a naturally sharp, acid level in the wine, it is filtered off its lees (the sediment formed by dead yeast cells) and is then rigorously protected against any future potential bacterial invasion. Red wines almost always undergo malolactic fermentation to soften them.

Blending Wines made from different grape varieties, or from various batches of the same crop that have been fermented separately, are often blended together to create a wine that is far greater than the sum of its individual parts. Many people believe that blended wines are inferior to varietal wines (the term that describes those crafted from a single grape variety), but this isn't the case. The famous Châteauneuf-du-Pape red wine of southern Rhône is a prime example of a blended wine that can be made up of 13 different grape varieties.

Oak ageing While everyday wines designed for immediate drinking are bottled as soon as they are ready – often within a matter of months – top wines (both red and white) are aged in oak barrels, generally of a 225-litre (50-gal.) capacity. Thanks to a magical marriage between the liquid and the wood, the wine mellows and becomes more complex, gaining extra dimensions of toasty, vanilla and spice flavours from the oak barrel over time. White wines are aged in barrel for around six to eight months, while red wines spend an average of nine to eighteen months in barrel.

THE ROLE OF OAK

In spite of many trials that have been undertaken with everything from acacia through eucalyptus to walnut, the extraordinary fact remains that oak is the only tree that is exploited in top-quality winemaking. No other type of wood has demonstrated such a natural affinity with wine.

Oak is strong, supple and watertight, and is used to assemble the barrels in which top wines are fermented and/or matured. The marriage between the wine and the wood is magical. The wine saps tannin, flavour and colour from the oak, and because the wood is porous, it allows the wine to breathe, causing further complex changes to its chemical make-up.

Oaked wines are well rounded, creamy and full-bodied, with unmistakable aromas and flavours of vanilla, hot-buttered toast and spice. These attributes are influenced by the age of the wood and the size of the barrel – brand-new and/or small barrels contribute even toastier notes – and the longer the time the wine spends in it, the greater the power the oak flavour will have.

The most prized oak comes from the French forests of Alliers, Limousin, Nevers, Tronçais and Vosges. Where and how the staves of wood are seasoned is also pivotal, as is the degree of charring the inside of the barrel receives when it is being constructed.

NB Descriptions of how rosé and champagne wines are produced can be found on pages 98 and 178 respectively.

Label lingo

'Appellation Bourgogne Contrôlée'

You will see plenty of bottles bearing the somewhat official-looking words 'Appellation Contrôlée' (shortened to AC), or Appellation d'Origine Contrôlée (AOC). This is indeed official because it means 'controlled appellation' and officially guarantees the official origin of a wine – in practice, this means where the grapes were grown – and, also, that official minimum standards are met when the wine is being made. Furthermore, this complicated and stringent slice of French wine law dictates which grape varieties are grown where, controls the yield of grapes per hectare or acre (grape by grape, place by place) and governs a whole host of other regulatory stuff. Confused? To put it simply, it says where the grapes were grown.

An AC can envelop a whole region – as in the example here. Appellation Bourgogne Contrôlée covers the whole of Burgundy and means that the grapes that make the wine can come from anywhere within the official wine region. Alternatively, an AC might embrace a collection of villages that are considered by the powers-that-be to produce better-quality grapes (and, with a bit of luck, better-quality wine). Then you have the villages that produce wines so good that they are allowed their own appellation. Finally, some individual vineyards carry their own name in the AC. These are the kind of wines that fetch fabulous prices at auction.

By now you might be thinking that appellation-contrôlée wines must be something really special. Some wish. Yes, the AC guarantees the origin, but it doesn't promise delivery of a tasty glass of wine each and every time, sorry to say. Some very mean stuff gets through with an AC label because local tasting panels (which are made up of local winemakers) are unwilling to throw out wines – it might be something they made themselves, after all.

'Chardonnay'

This is the name of the grape used to make this wine. It is extremely unusual (and very often illegal under local French wine laws) for appellation-contrôlée wine labels to show the name of grape varieties.

'Elevé et mis en bouteille par Louis Jadot, Beaune, France'

This literally translates as 'raised and put in bottle by Louis Jadot' in the town of Beaune in France. In other words, Louis Jadot is the name of the Beaune-based company that blended, matured and bottled the wine.

'Fondée en 1859'

This means 'Founded in 1859'.

'75cl e'

The contents of the bottle. The 'e' means that the bottle size is approved under European Union regulations.

'13% vol.'

The alcoholic strength of the wine expressed as a percentage of the total volume of the bottle.

More French Label Lore

Blanc white.

Blanc de Blancs a white wine made entirely from white grapes.

Blanc de Noirs a white wine made entirely from black grapes.

Brut dry sparkling wines.

Cave (coopérative) a co-operative winery.

Château a wine estate (especially in Bordeaux).

Claret the generic English name for red Bordeaux wines.

Côte(s) and Coteau(x) generally superior wines made from grapes grown on hillside sites. Most of the best vineyard sites are indeed on hillsides – but not all: the 'Côtes du Rhône' name covers just about every wine in the Rhône valley! They just thought it sounded smart to say 'Côtes du Rhône' and not just 'Rhône'.

Crémant traditional-method fizz from regions other than Champagne.

Cru literally 'growth', meaning a vineyard or group of vineyards of superior quality

Cru Classé 'classed growth'. Applies to top Bordeaux wines.

Cuvée the contents of a vat, a blend or a special batch of wine.

Demi-Sec medium dry.

Domaine a wine estate, especially in Burgundy.

Doux sweet.

CHATEAU

1958 1794

GADET-St JULIEN

CRU

EMILION

CONTROLEE

945

AU CHATEAU

PROPRIETAIRE

Extra-Dry a style of champagne that is sweeter than Brut.

Grand Cru literally 'great growth', usually meaning the best vineyards in a region. Some regions, such as Burgundy, are very strict. But in St-Emilion, 60 per cent of vineyards are Grand Cru, so it doesn't mean very much here.

Liquoreux very sweet.

Mas a wine estate, especially in the south of France.

Mis (en bouteille) au Château/Domaine/La Propriété estate-bottled.

Monopole a vineyard wholly owned by a producer.

Mousseux sparkling.

Non-Vintage a blend of wines from the grape harvest of more than one year. Commonly used in champagne.

Nouveau new wine.

Pétillant semi-sparkling.

Premier Cru literally 'first growth', used to describe superior wine villages, vineyard sites or the wines themselves. But, irritatingly, in Champagne and Burgundy 'first' doesn't mean best. Their top wines are Grands Crus – Great Growths. Don't expect the French to make their regulations easy for us to understand. That wouldn't be French!

Rosé pink.

Rouge red.

Sec dry still wines.

Supérieur wines possessing a slightly higher alcohol content than is normal for any given appellation. It does not mean that they are superior in taste, however!

Sur Lie wines that are bottled directly from their yeast sediment (called lees) without filtering, which adds freshness and creaminess to the wine.

Vieilles Vignes old vines.

Vin Délimité de Qualité Supérieur (VDQS) delimited wine of superior quality. Well, not really. This is the next tier down in the classification system to appellation contrôlée. Hardly any wines are VDQS and they'll probably scrap the whole tier soon.

Vin de Pays country wines that are often full of character and, usually, offer great value for money.

Vin de Table table wine. The basic stuff. Plonk.

How to taste

When we're drinking wine, it's terribly easy to let the liquid simply slip down our throats without giving it much thought. But if you make a conscious effort to evaluate the wine you're drinking, you'll very quickly find that you are able to judge a wine much more accurately as you build up a mental library of smells and flavours. Make some notes because the human memory for taste is not very reliable – taste may sometimes be very hard to describe, but it's certainly far, far more difficult to recall.

Look Wine shouldn't have anything strange bits floating in it and be suspicious if it's cloudy. The wine's appearance also gives hints about its age and style. Simple, young, dry white wines are very pale in colour, often possessing a slightly green tinge; richer or more mature styles have a golden tinge; and many sweet white wines are deep gold. Conversely, red wines fade in colour as they age: young reds have a purple hue, turning from ruby to garnet to tawny. Full-bodied, complex styles are very dense and you won't be able to see through the wine, but if you can spy the bottom of the glass, it indicates that it is light-bodied.
Smell Taking the time to smell the wine properly is hugely important because the nerve endings that detect flavour are located in the upper nasal cavity and not in the mouth, contrary to what all of us perceive. Gently swirl the wine around the glass to release the aroma. Ideally, the glass shouldn't be more than half full so that you can do this more easily – this can be a very sloppy business – and it leaves enough room for you to be able to stick your nose in for a proper sniff. What you are detecting here is the character of the grape variety and it is very useful to compare the aroma of the wine with something familiar to you – for example, it may remind you of strawberries or newly mown grass. As you gain experience, you'll be surprised by how quickly you'll be able to recognize different grape varieties simply from the smell of the wine. It's truly thrilling when you find that you can achieve this. Incidentally, if the wine smells musty, vinegary, sulphurous or vegetal, it is probably faulty.
Taste Take a small sip of the wine now and gargle it around your mouth, allowing the liquid to reach all the parts of your mouth. If you can,

simultaneously suck in a little air. This is the way to enjoy the full flavour of a wine. By the way, flavour in this context is not the same as taste: what the mouth identifies are things like sweetness, acidity and the body of the wine – it is your nose that it is doing all the work in sending the flavour messages to your brain.

Afterthoughts After you've swallowed the wine, think about how long the taste lingers in your mouth – this is known as the wine's finish or length. Was the wine in balance? A balanced wine is when acidity, fruit, tannin and alcohol are in perfect harmony. To look at these factors in more detail: a wine high in natural acidity tastes sherbety; if the wine is very fruity, it suggests that it's young (wines mellow as they age); wine containing a lot of tannin causes your mouth to pucker up and feel dry; and the effect of alcohol makes your mouth feel hot and oily. Did it have an oaky taste, which suggests that the wine has been fermented and/or aged in oak barrels?

Common wine faults

Corked wine It is easy to spot a corked wine by its smell alone – it reeks of old mushrooms, damp garden sheds and muddy football socks. If you identify this pong – and it would be hard not to – always send/take back the wine because it will be undrinkable. The problem is caused by a compound called 2,4,6-Trichloroanisole (shortened to TCA) that can taint natural cork and it is estimated that as many as one in 15 bottles of wine sealed with a natural cork may be affected by TCA.

This problem would be eliminated overnight if every bottle of wine were sealed with a screwtop or synthetic cork. While the latter still provides the romance and tradition of extracting a cork from a bottle, they are not ideal because they don't always form a snug fit and the wine can leak away – and when the converse is true, it can be an almighty struggle to get the cork out at all. Screwtops, therefore, offer an ideal solution all round and are becoming more and more popular with winemakers around the world – virtually all of New Zealand's white wines are now sealed in this way, for example. In fact, white wines that come with a screwtop are fresher, fruitier and more aromatic than

their cork-sealed counterparts. Trials are under way to test the effect of screwtops on wines that need to be bottle-aged (that is, bottled wine that isn't drinkable unless it has been tucked away for a number of years), but it appears as if screwtops are absolutely fine for any wine of any colour that is made to be drunk within a year or so of bottling. In France, the whole idea of screwtops is met with a 'Quel horreur!' (What horror!) attitude and only the most innovative producers use them (for example, Yvon Mau in Bordeaux of all places, one of the most traditional, dyed-in-the-wool wine regions of France).

Oxidized wine This happens when the wine has absorbed too much oxygen, usually because the cork has dried out and air has crept in to attack the wine. This is why it's so important to keep bottles sealed with a cork on their sides. Oxidized wines smell – and often taste – of sherry.

Tartrate crystals Don't worry if you see sugar-like crystals in your glass, on the cork or even in the wine itself. These odourless and tasteless deposits are a natural precipitation of tartaric acid and won't do you or the wine any harm. In fact, they're a very good sign that the wine hasn't been over-manipulated.

25

CHAPTER 1 **BORDEAUX**

Henry Plantagenet, the future Henry II of England, was on to a good thing when he married Eleanor of Aquitaine in 1152 for she brought as part of her dowry the province of Bordeaux in the southwest of France. This effectively ceded the region to the English crown and marked the beginning of a relationship between Bordeaux and Britain that has influenced and shaped the UK's wine-drinking habits ever since. Indeed, as a nation we've been drinking Bordeaux wines for so many centuries now that the red wine has even earned its own English name: claret.

THE ORIGIN OF THE CLARET NAME
It seems strange to think of it now, but in the past all Bordeaux red wines used to be made in a light-bodied style with a very pale colour – almost verging on a rosé wine, in fact. This was – and still is – called 'clairet', so it isn't difficult to see how the word 'claret' entered into the English language.

With over 10,000 producers making an average of 850 million bottles of wine a year from 120,630 ha (298,088 acres) of vines, this is not only France's largest fine-wine-producing region but is arguably also the world's greatest wine region. Close proximity to the Atlantic and an enormous diversity of mesoclimates – the distinct and different climates of small areas as opposed to the general climate of the whole region – and soils allow Bordeaux to make a wide range of wines: from grassy, aromatic, dry whites to golden sweet whites, from intense, blackcurranty reds via summer-fruited rosés to crisp sparkling whites. Blending key grape varieties is important in maintaining Bordeaux's unique, benchmark character. Cabernet Sauvignon, Merlot and Cabernet Franc are the principal grape varieties used for red and rosé wines, while Sauvignon Blanc and Sémillon are the most important white-grape varieties.

The landscape is rather flat and uninspiring on the whole, the exception being the gentle sand and limestone hills to the northeast and east. The whole is trisected by the rivers Garonne and Dordogne, which meet north of the historic city of Bordeaux to flow into the sea as the Gironde – and the best vineyards are those situated closest to these rivers. The climate is temperate Atlantic Maritime, though the region is protected from the effects of the harsh, wet and salty prevailing southwesterly winds by the sand dunes and the pine forests of the Landes to the west and south of the Gironde estuary. Then there is the warming Gulf Stream that crucially raises the temperature near the coast. As a result, the summers are usually long and warm, and winters relatively mild. Even so, it's sometimes so cool and wet in the autumn that the grapes struggle to ripen fully.

The Bordeaux winemakers believe passionately that 'terroir' (the vineyard's unique 'address', reflecting the interaction between its soil, topography, climate and exposure to the sun) determines the style and pedigree of the wine and, to a large extent, the boundaries of the region's sub-divisions have been drawn up by soil type. Incidentally, you may come across the terms Right Bank and Left Bank. East of the river Dordogne, the vineyards of St-Emilion, Pomerol and Fronsac form the Right Bank area; west of the rivers Garonne and Gironde is the Left Bank area that includes the Médoc, Graves and Sauternes. There is a large area called Entre-Deux-Mers ('between the two seas') that lies between the tidal Dordogne and Garonne rivers (hence its name).

Basic Bordeaux

For all the hype surrounding the very top wines of Bordeaux, such as the legendary names of Château Latour and Château Lafite-Rothschild, the vast majority of production is pretty ordinary stuff, most especially when it comes to the red wines. Indeed, in cool years, inexpensive, basic Bordeaux reds can be horrible wines, tasting green, stalky and tannic because the grapes haven't ripened successfully. The cold, damp climate means that growers often live on a knife-edge at harvest time – will the grapes have ripened sufficiently?

The basic white wines, labelled Bordeaux Blanc, are a much better bet than the reds. To guarantee a dry style, look for labels bearing the words Bordeaux Sec or Vin Sec de Bordeaux – or, better still, find one that has Sauvignon Blanc written on it (this indicates that the wine has been made from the Sauvignon Blanc grape variety only).

The rosé wines of Bordeaux can be pleasant, with aromas and flavours of cream, plums, wild strawberries, and other hedgerow fruits.

TASTING NOTES

Château St-Germain, Bordeaux Supérieur, 2004
Oz says: Full-bodied, with dark cherry fruit, but it also boasts a creamy texture. This is a pretty good basic claret – chewy, earthy, dry and crying out for a sirloin steak.
James says: There's far too much petrol in there.

Classic blends

As the famous, top-class wines of Bordeaux prove, wines made from a blend of different grape varieties are not inferior to varietal wines (the term that describes those crafted from a single grape variety). Here, red wines (which account for 85 per cent of production) are created from a mix of Cabernet Sauvignon, Merlot, Cabernet Franc and, sometimes, Petit Verdot and Malbec, the proportion of each grape variety varying from commune to commune. As a general rule, though, you can expect the wines that come from the left-hand side of the Gironde estuary to be dominated by Cabernet Sauvignon, while it is Merlot that rules across the river. Sauvignon Blanc, Sémillon and, sometimes, Muscadelle (which is no relation to the Muscat grape variety) form the basis of both the dry and sweet white wines of Bordeaux. Simple, inexpensive wines are made for drinking as soon as they are released, but the finest of both reds and whites can be extremely long-lived.

Cabernet Sauvignon is possibly the world's most famous red-grape variety that everyone has heard of and Bordeaux alone accounts for a whopping 33 per cent of world production. It needs to be planted

This place grows the most expensive wine in the Medoc – a couple of hundred quid a bottle. But we were perfectly satisfied with the £80 bottles from their neighbours.

THE BORDEAUX WINE TRADE
Bordeaux is full of middlemen. Producers do not sell direct to their customers (whether it be wine in bulk or wine in bottle). Instead, they trade with one of the 400 'négociants' or merchant houses (see page 139) that in turn sell to the importers abroad or the distributors at home. However, the producer doesn't deal directly with the négociant, either. They strike their deals via one of the 130 'courtiers en vins' (wine-brokers).

34

somewhere sunny and hot if it's to ripen fully and when it does, it contributes a host of fabulous flavours to the blend – blackcurrants, cherry, blackberry, chocolate and green pepper – and as the wine ages, a fragrance of cedar, pencil shavings and cigar box. It's also high in tannin, which not only provides the backbone to the wine but also acts as a natural preservative (the higher the tannin level, the longer the wine can age). Cabernet Sauvignon performs best on the gravel banks of the left bank of the river Gironde.

Merlot is the most widely planted red-grape variety in Bordeaux (the world's leading producer of this variety). It ripens earlier than Cabernet Sauvignon and makes wines that ooze mellow, supple flavours of plump brambles, damsons, blackcurrants, chocolate, black cherries, pepper, fruitcake and roasted coffee beans – and sometimes there's a trace of cigar-box aroma and a taste of mint. In Bordeaux, it is used to flesh out and soften the more austere Cabernet Sauvignon. It grows best on clay soils, most especially in the Pomerol appellation (the word used to describe the official, delimited grape-growing area of a region or a district – see page 18 for further information).

Cabernet Franc adds perfume and a slightly earthy and grassy quality to the blend alongside flavours of raspberries, redcurrants and blackcurrants. Cabernet Franc thrives in the cool soils of St-Emilion and Pomerol.

Sémillon is the most important white-grape variety of Bordeaux, most particularly in Graves and Sauternes. When it's blended with Sauvignon Blanc, the wine it makes boasts aromas and flavours of pears, apricots and peaches when it is young. Leave it to age, however, and it becomes lanolin-soft, honeyed, custardy and nutty. The greatest asset of the thick-skinned Sémillon, however, is its susceptibility to 'noble rot' (see page 56). This gives concentrated, very sweet juice, which in turn creates lusciously sweet wine. It is therefore a crucial ingredient in Bordeaux's sweet wines.

Sauvignon Blanc makes bone-dry wines with grassy, appley flavours. While there are some 100 per cent Sauvignon Blanc wines in Bordeaux, it is usually blended with Sémillon, to which it adds a vital streak of mouth-watering acidity, whether the wine is dry or sweet in style.

Getting to grips with the classifications

The Bordeaux region is split into sub-regions, which in turn are divided into districts known as communes. Within these lie the individual vineyard properties that usually take the name of a château – and some of them really are châteaux, the magnificent, moated, towered and turreted houses that reek of grandeur and tradition.

Like all appellation-contrôlée wines (see page 18), the name on the label guarantees the source of the wine – and there are 57 appellations in total here. Any wine (red, white, rosé or sparkling) labelled Appellation Bordeaux Contrôlée can be made from grapes grown anywhere within the region, but while perfectly drinkable, on the whole, it is unlikely to be a great wine. Also, when you see Bordeaux Supérieur on a label don't be hoodwinked into thinking that it's always going to be a better wine; it simply means that the wine has a slightly higher content of alcohol. Having said that, some of these wines are in fact superior, mainly because they are required under local wine laws to have been matured for a longer period compared with basic Bordeaux. Almost all of the petits châteaux – the generic term for Bordeaux's mass of unclassified châteaux wines – are labelled Bordeaux Supérieur and many of these offer excellent value.

The next level up in the hierarchy is the more specific appellations covering the sub-regions, such as Haut-Médoc and Entre-Deux-Mers. Often, the appellation contrôlée for these covers one colour of wine only. Hopping up another rung of the quality ladder come the individual communes or villages, such as Pomerol and Margaux. This is as refined as the Bordeaux appellation-contrôlée structure gets, but, hang on to your hats because there are further quality classifications.

The single-estate Crus Bourgeois ('Bourgeois' Growths) from the Médoc peninsula form the next rung up and there are 247 of these, further classified into Crus Bourgeois Exceptionnels, Crus Bourgeois Supérieur and Crus Bourgeois. At the top of the ladder, the finest wines are known as Crus Classés (Classed Growths). Congratulations if you've kept up so far, but take a deep breath because even the Crus Classés are sub-divided.

In 1855, the Bordeaux Chamber of Commerce was commissioned by the organizers of the Paris Exposition to produce a tiered classification system – the aforementioned Crus Classés – of the Bordeaux châteaux. While the list that was drawn up categorized each château in order of the prices that were being charged for their wines at the time, the classification nevertheless reflected the relative quality and popularity of the châteaux, and give or take a few nudges here and there, hasn't changed since and is still very important in driving the prices fetched by the very top wines today.

In the Médoc sub-region, the finest châteaux are ranked into five groups, from Premier Grand Cru Classé (First Class Growth) to Cinquième Grand Cru Classé (Fifth Class Growth) – and, unlike some other parts of France, Premier does mean the best, just for once.

Across the river in the St-Emilion sub-region, however, the classification system is (somewhat annoyingly) slightly different, probably because it was devised 100 years later (and is reviewed every ten years or so on average). The basic wines are simply labelled St-Emilion. But (here we go again) four communes (or 'satellites', as they are called here) – Lussac, Montagne, Puisseguin and St-Georges – can append their own names to the label (Puisseguin-St-Emilion, for example). Then there are the St-Emilion Grands Crus, but this doesn't

Under the rules of the 35-hour French working week, the vinter is not allowed to drive his tractor after Thursday lunchtime. Clearly this ruling does not apply to his children.

mean much because producers only have to lower the grape yields and increase the minimum alcohol levels to qualify for Grand Cru status – indeed, 60 per cent of St-Emilion's vineyards are Grands Crus. The top châteaux are classified in a two-tier system: St-Emilion Grand Cru Classé and St-Emilion Premier Grand Cru Classé, though the latter are further divided into grade A and grade B. There are only two grade-A châteaux (Château Cheval Blanc and Château Ausone) and 11 B-grade châteaux, including Château Angélus and Château Beau-Séjour Bécot, which were promoted in the latest classification in 1996.

Now take another big breath. There is no classification system in Pomerol. In Graves, however, the finest wines are entitled to call themselves Grand Cru Classé de Graves – except that these Classed Growths are all located in the neighbouring, but separate, Pessac-Léognan appellation. All will become clear later on in this chapter. Finally (phew), the top châteaux of the five Sauternes communes are divided into just three categories – Premier Cru Supérieur, Premier Cru and Deuxième Cru. Château d'Yquem is the only château to hold the top Premier Cru Supérieur status. You deserve a large glass of wine if you've managed to make head or tail of all this.

BORDEAUX'S 'SECOND' WINES
When you see the words 'Grand Vin' on a label, it doesn't refer to the quality of the wine. What it means is that the bottle contains the main wine of a château, identified simply by the name of the château. Some châteaux produce what is known as a second wine, made either from the fruit of young vines, or from wine that isn't up to scratch for the Grand Vin. Some of these offer good value, but choose with care. Unfortunately, the labels of these second wines do not tell you that this is what they are. For example, there is nothing on the label of Château Petit-Mouton to advise you that this is the second wine of Château Mouton-Rothschild. You will therefore have to do some advance detective work if these are the wines you wish to buy.

VINTAGE VARIATION
The quality of Bordeaux wines varies from year to year according to the weather, so always seek professional advice from a respected wine merchant before buying expensive wine, most especially if you are purchasing it for investment purposes.

The Médoc

The Médoc peninsula on the gravelly left bank of the Gironde, the heartland of the Cabernet Sauvignon grape variety, is divided into the sub-regions of the Médoc (with wines that can be dismissed on the whole because they are mostly rather boring and one-dimensional) and the far superior Haut-Médoc that occupies the southern half of the peninsula. This runs from the outskirts of the city of Bordeaux up to St-Seurin-de-Cadourne. Almost all of the Médoc's gravel is found in the southern half and this is where you will find the world-renowned red-wine communes of Margaux, St-Julien, Pauillac, St-Estèphe (each boasting myriad Crus Classés), Listrac-Médoc and Moulis. The 4500 ha (11,115 acres) of vineyards not covered by these six communal appellations is labelled Haut-Médoc and includes many good value Crus Bourgeois wines – in fact, 71 per cent of the wine produced here comes from a Cru Bourgeois property.

There's an old Médoc saying that 'vines like to see the water, but not get their feet wet'. When you see how close some of the vines get to the muddy edge of the river, it's not surprising that hearts are fluttering at thoughts of the impact of global warming. Most of the top vineyards, however, are situated between 4 metres (13 ft) and 29 metres (95 ft) above sea level. Incidentally, the very name Médoc comes from the Latin *medio aquae* meaning 'in the middle of the water' – and you only have to look at a map of the region to see how this came about because the Médoc is wedged between the waves of the Atlantic and the wide expanse of the Gironde estuary, the largest in Europe.

Vines not only benefit from the milder climate that accompanies large expanses of water but also prefer well-drained sites. This is why the ridges of gravelly soils found here are so desirable, because the rain runs almost straight through them. It makes the roots of the vine dig deep for water and nutrients, which is beneficial in years of drought. Gravel also stores the heat of the sun during the day that is then released long into the night, a factor of paramount importance given Bordeaux's generally cool and damp climate. But enough talk of climate and soils; it's time to journey through the Promised Land.

Chateau Palmer: we could have stayed here and drunk its delicious expensive wine, but we decided to camp instead.

The Médoc wine road (route D2) is one that any wine lover must drive along at least once in his or her lifetime (or, preferably, with all this wine, be driven). Unfortunately, very few of the top châteaux welcome visitors except by appointment and there's hardly any of the razzamatazz of visitor centres, self-guided tours, shops, picnic areas and so on that are ten a penny in somewhere like the Napa Valley in California. Don't let this put you off, though, because there's still plenty to see – and taste. Just check where is open when with the tourist office in Bordeaux before you set off and they can also help make appointments where necessary.

Having left the city of Bordeaux, the first commune you will reach is Margaux. This appellation is pretty big at 1525 ha (3768 acres) and is spread through the villages of Margaux, Arsac, Cantenac, Labarde and Soussans. All of the vines, however, are grown on banks of gravel and there are no fewer than 21 Crus Classés here. The wines from the best properties can be singled out by their divine perfume of sweet blackcurrants, plums, violets, cedar wood, vanilla and roasted nuts. Unfortunately, the quality of Margaux wines took a dip in the last half of the twentieth century, but this decline has been reversed of late thanks to new ownership and a new generation, and the wines are now beginning to claw back their reputation as some of the finest in the world.

By the way, Margaux is only a short distance northwest of the villages of Macau and St-Christoly where, in spring, they catch shad, a large herring-like fish weighing up to 3 kg (6.6 lb). Believe it or not, it cannot live anywhere else. The downside to eating this fish is that it's incredibly bony – but it does have a wonderful, delicate taste. Look for alose à l'oseille, which is shad marinated in oil and wine and then baked with a stuffing made of shad roe and sorrel sautéed in butter (the sorrel helps to disintegrate the bones).

Continuing northward brings you to the commune of St-Julien. This may not take up much space relatively speaking (921 ha/2276 acres), but no fewer than 11 Crus Classés occupy 85 per cent of the land, thanks to the gravelly outcrops that Cabernet Sauvignon vines love so much. The wine that is created here has a beautiful cedary scent and has the perfect balance between fruit and tannin: this is quintessential red Bordeaux.

Like St-Julien, its neighbour of Pauillac is another jewel in the crown of the Haut-Médoc, indeed of the whole of the Bordeaux region. This is where the Cabernet Sauvignon grape variety is king and this is where you'll find the great wine names of Château Latour, Château Lafite-Rothschild and Château Mouton-Rothschild (all Premiers Grands Crus Classés; the commune has a further 15 Cru Classé estates) that create the kind of wines that every ambitious Cabernet Sauvignon winemaker around the world dreams of emulating. And dream on they will because no-one has quite been able to duplicate these powerful, long-lived wines that are packed with blackcurrant flavour and are heady with the

CHÂTEAU D'ANGLUDET, CRU BOURGEOIS, MARGAUX
The English Sichel family (who are part-owners of Château Palmer, also in Margaux) consistently make a marvellous red wine at this homely, 34-ha (84-acre) château located in the backwoods of Margaux. It's so fruity and gentle – all juicy, soft blackcurrants and blackberries – that you want to drink it as soon as it's released, yet it ages very well for up to a decade or more. The best bit of all is that it's wine of Cru Classé quality without the Cru Classé price tag.

fragrance of cedar and cigar boxes. The vines grow close to the estuary on deep gravel banks that surround the sleepy town of Pauillac, home to the commune's Maison du Vin that sells the local wine and, theoretically, where you can fix up appointments to visit the châteaux. Each commune has one of these centres, but they are not always the best place to buy wine (they are generally over-priced).

If you're feeling peckish, you must try the tender Pauillac lamb, raised on its mother's milk for 60 days before being turned out to grass on the salt marshes. In the times of seasonal herd migration, the sheep breeders had an arrangement with the owners of the Médoc wine châteaux. After the grape harvest, the sheep would be brought in to graze among the vines. This kept everyone happy: the shepherds had a source of free food for their flocks, while the château owner benefited from a free weed-removal and fertilizing service. You can sometimes still spot sheep in the vineyards even today.

There's also entrecôte Bordelaise, a boned rib steak (preferably from the flavoursome local Bazas beef) that, ideally, should be grilled over smoking vine twigs and then topped with a generous portion of shallots, parsley and cèpes (succulent, brown-capped, fat-stemmed wild mushrooms). Apparently, in the olden days rats provided the meat for this dish, said to have been very tasty.

TASTING NOTES
Château d'Angludet, Margaux, 1999

Oz says: This is quite full, dry and balanced. It's slightly earthy, there's soft dark fruit and it even has a little herb rasp. But it has no perfume and it isn't elegant. It's attractive enough for a claret lover, but not if you don't like claret.
James says: A rather boring wine. There's a bit of heat in it and I don't want to get this in my eye, I think.

**CHÂTEAU PICHON-LONGUEVILLE,
DEUXIÈME GRAND CRU CLASSÉ, PAUILLAC**
This fairy-tale, Disneyesque château dating
from 1851 (it was built by Baron Joseph de Pichon-
Longueville) is now owned by AXA-Millésimes,
part of the giant AXA insurance group.

Much money has been thrown at this property
and, under the direction of the enthusiastic
Christian Seely, the château itself has been
beautifully and tastefully restored, and a new,
state-of-the-art winery has been constructed.
Its wines are almost as good as Pauillac's First
Growths and should be cellared for at least ten
years, although they're likely to keep for 30.
The second wine is les Tourelles de Pichon.

AXA-Millésimes also own Château Petit-Village
(in Pomerol), Château Suduirat (in Sauternes)
and Pibran (in Pauillac).

**CHÂTEAU MOUTON-ROTHSCHILD,
PREMIER GRAND CRU CLASSÉ, PAUILLAC**
In 1973, this estate was promoted from Second
Growth to First Growth status, an unprecedented
move and the only time it has ever happened. This
was the result of the extraordinary, pioneering
efforts of the late Baron Philippe de Rothschild,
who inherited this run-down, 75-ha (185-acre)
property in 1922 at the age of 20 and turned it into
one of the most famous names in the wine world.

The vineyards are located on perfectly situated
gravel banks and thus a high proportion of
Cabernet Sauvignon is grown to give a wine that in
most years teems with rich blackcurrant flavours
and heady cigar-box fragrances. It's a superb wine
that needs to be tucked away for at least ten years
before it is ready to drink and it's a great collector's
item. Indeed, some people buy the wine solely for
its artist-designed label. Since 1945, every vintage
has had a different label, created by some of the
most famous names of the art world, such as
Marc Chagall, Salvador Dalí, Pablo Picasso and
Andy Warhol.

The second wine is called Château Petit-Mouton
and there is a small amount of Château Aile
d'Argent, a white wine that would be fabulous
drunk with the local oysters. But Mouton-
Rothschild is also linked with the Mouton Cadet
red, white and rosé wines, initially made from the
estate's grapes, but now made from grapes
sourced throughout the region, which
demonstrates what can be achieved with a wine
brand if it's marketed successfully: Mouton Cadet
Rouge is the world's most widely sold red Bordeaux
with yearly sales of 15 million bottles. When you
taste it, though, you might ask yourself why.
There's nothing wrong with it, but it's not
particularly exciting. Far more inspirational
at this level are Dourthe Numéro 1 Blanc and
Yvon Mau's Premius and Exigence brands.

Furthest north in the Haut-Médoc, you'll come to the more rural-feeling commune of St-Estèphe, and wines that don't command such high prices (in as far as it's the least highly priced of the top Haut-Médoc wines). One of the reasons behind this is that many of the estates weren't in existence at the time of the 1855 classification and were therefore never classified – indeed, there are only five Crus Classés in this commune. If the same classification were to be re-enacted today, some non-classified estates – and Château Haut-Marbuzet provides a fine example here – would probably be awarded Cru Classé status because their wines deserve it. Mind you, there is less gravel in this large, 1265-ha (3126-acre) commune and it's cooler, so Cabernet Sauvignon doesn't fare so well here and the grapes ripen a week later than those in Margaux. This can give wines that are pretty tough in style owing to their high level of tannins and, as a result, you need to stash them away for a long period (ten to 20 years) before they are ready to drink.

St-Estèphe is also famous for its eels. Indeed, the people of Bordeaux seem to have a weakness for these slippery creatures, preferably sautéed in parsley and garlic, and they turn up on menus throughout the Bordeaux region. Young eels, called pibales, are now sold for almost as much as caviare because poachers have ensured that this delicacy has become rare. Caviare, by the way, is produced in several fish farms in the Gironde.

While mentioning eels, another Bordeaux speciality is lamprey, an almost meaty, eel-like type of sea snake that is found in the estuaries of large rivers. Like salmon, they swim upstream to spawn and so they are easily trapped. It's a rather scary-looking creature (it's a cyclostome, so it has a jawless, fixed-open mouth, toothed and funnel-like) and, like a giant leech, lives by attaching itself to large fish to suck out their tissues and blood. Yes, people really eat these. For the classic lamproie à la Bordelaise – and be warned that it's one of those love-it-or-loathe-it dishes – the lampreys are stewed for four or five hours in red wine, leeks, mushrooms, shallots and chopped ham. Towards the end of the cooking time, the sauce is thickened with the blood of the lamprey that is drained off beforehand. In the old days, they used to collect the blood simply by nailing the live lampreys to a wall and letting them bleed to death.

Then there is the tricky business of removing the poisonous, cartilaginous cord that runs down the lamprey's back. It is said that Henry I died of a surfeit of lampreys, but perhaps he just ingested a piece of that cord.

It's time to turn inland to the vineyards of Listrac-Médoc. These don't see the river because they are situated a short distance into the Landes forest and they are also a little higher, so it's much cooler. There isn't much gravel here, either. All in all, the wines lack the class of those made nearer the water, with a chunkier, earthier character. But now that more Merlot is being planted (because it has a greater chance of ripening here), the wines are improving with each vintage – 2003 was pretty good. Meanwhile, its neighbour, Moulis, is the smallest commune in the Haut-Médoc (with only 550 ha (1359 acres) of vineyards), but, crucially, it possesses a ridge of gravel where Cabernet Sauvignon ripens fully. When you try these smooth, fruity wines (and make a point of choosing the Crus Bourgeois) you might find yourself pleasantly surprised at the relatively reasonable prices that are being asked for them (compared with their Haut-Médoc cousins, that is).

TASTING NOTES
Sainsbury's Taste The Difference Margaux, 2002
Oz says: A full, meaty nose. In flavour, it has some nuts and bone-dry, soft dark fruit. It's not exciting – it has no focus – but it's a reasonable drink. It's far too expensive, though, for what is merely a decent dry red wine, not a masterpiece.
James says: I don't know what to think about this wine. There might be a bit of liquorice. It's too acidic and there's a bit of hairspray in it as if someone sprayed their hair in the vineyard and it got into the wine.

THE UPDATED 1855 RED-WINE CLASSIFICATION OF MÉDOC RED WINES

PREMIERS GRANDS CRUS CLASSÉS:
Lafite-Rothschild (Pauillac), Latour (Pauillac), Margaux (Margaux) and Mouton-Rothschild (Pauillac).

DEUXIÈMES GRANDS CRUS CLASSÉS:
Brane-Cantenac (Margaux), Cos d'Estournel (St-Estèphe), Ducru-Beaucaillou (St-Julien), Durfort-Vivens (Margaux), Gruaud-Larose (St-Julien), Lascombes (Margaux), Léoville-Barton (St-Julien), Léoville-Las-Cases (St-Julien), Léoville-Poyferré (St-Julien), Montrose (St-Estèphe), Pichon-Longueville (Pauillac), Pichon-Longueville-Comtesse-de-Lalande (Pauillac), Rauzan-Gassies (Margaux) and Rauzan-Segla (Margaux).

TROISIÈMES GRANDS CRUS CLASSÉS:
Boyd-Cantenac (Margaux), Calon-Ségur (St-Estèphe), Cantenac-Brown (Margaux), Desmirail (Margaux), Ferrière (Margaux), Giscours (Margaux), d'Issan (Margaux), Kirwan (Margaux), Lagrange (St-Julien), la Lagune (Haut-Médoc), Langoa-Barton (St-Julien), Malescot St-Exupéry (Margaux), Marquis d'Alesme-Becker (Margaux) and Palmer (Margaux).

QUATRIÈMES GRANDS CRUS CLASSÉS:
Beychevelle (St-Julien), Branaire-Ducru (St-Julien), Duhart-Milon-Rothschild (Pauillac), Lafon-Rochet (St-Estèphe), Marquis-de-Terme (Margaux), Pouget (Margaux), Prieuré-Lichine (Margaux), St-Pierre (St-Julien), Talbot (St-Julien) and la Tour-Carnet (Haut-Médoc).

CINQUIÈMES GRANDS CRUS CLASSÉS:
d'Armailhac (Pauillac), Batailley (Pauillac), Belgrave (Haut-Médoc), Camensac (Haut-Médoc), Cantemerle (Haut-Médoc), Clerc-Milon (Pauillac), Cos-Labory (St-Estèphe), Croizet-Bages (Pauillac), Dauzac (Margaux), Grand-Puy-Ducasse (Pauillac), Grand-Puy-Lacoste (Pauillac), Haut-Bages-Libéral (Pauillac), Haut-Batailley (Pauillac), Lynch-Bages (Pauillac), Lynch-Moussas (Pauillac), Pédesclaux (Pauillac), Pontet-Canet (Pauillac) and du Tertre (Margaux).

The right-bank wines

The air is a little warmer on the right-hand side of the river Gironde and warmer still upstream along the river Dordogne, but the clay and limestone soils are colder than the gravels of the Médoc, so they are mostly planted with the earlier-maturing Merlot and Cabernet Franc grape varieties, which ripen on these soils where Cabernet Sauvignon would not.

No trip to the Bordeaux wine region would be complete without a visit to the captivating town of St-Emilion, which lies at the centre of the historic wine sub-region of the same name. The tourist office here can advise you of which châteaux are open to the public (or you can access this information via www.saint-emilion-tourisme.com). In total, there are 5682 ha (14,040 acres) under vine owned by 1000 different estates spread across eight different communes.

South of the town, steep slopes drop down from the edge of a limestone plateau to the Dordogne river. Vines have been cultivated on these slopes since Roman times, making it one of the oldest winemaking areas of Bordeaux. Even today, these are the vineyards that supply the grapes for all but two of St-Emilion's Premiers Grands Crus Classés (Château Cheval Blanc and Château Figeac are located on a ridge of gravel in an enclave west of the town, towards Libourne).

The relatively high percentage of the Merlot grape variety in the blend that creates the wines of St-Emilion makes them much easier to drink in some respects compared with the Cabernet Sauvignon-dominated reds of the left bank. The wine is relatively soft and has a touch of fruitcake sweetness about it that historically has always made it very popular with UK drinkers. By the way, this is the wine to drink with the local speciality of duck with prunes.

THE 1996 CLASSIFICATION OF ST-EMILION
PREMIERS GRANDS CRUS CLASSÉS:
A-grade: Ausone and Cheval Blanc
B-grade: Angélus, Beau-Séjour Bécot,
Beauséjour-Duffaut-Lagarrosse, Belair,
Canon, Clos Fourtet, Figeac, la Gaffelière,
Magdelaine, Pavie and Trottevieille.
GRANDS CRUS CLASSÉS:
L'Arrosée, Balestard la Tonnelle, Bellevue,
Bergat, Berliquet, Cadet-Bon, Cadet-Piola,
Canon la Gaffelière, Cap de Mourlin, Chauvin,
Clos des Jacobins, Clos de l'Oratoire, Clos
St-Martin, la Clotte, la Clusière, Corbin,
Corbin-Michotte, la Couspaude, Couvent des
Jacobins, Curé Bon, Dassault, la Dominique,
Faurie-de-Souchard, Fonplégade, Fonroque,
Franc Mayne, Grand Mayne, Grand Pontet,
Les Grandes Murailles, Guadet St-Julien,
Haut Corbin, Haut Sarpe, Lamarzelle, Laniote,
Larcis Ducasse, Larmande, Laroque, Laroze,
Matras, Moulin du Cadet, Pavie Decesse, Pavie
Macquin, Petit Faurie de Soutard, le Prieuré,
Ripeau, St-Georges Côte Pavie, la Serre, Soutard,
Tertre Daugay, la Tour du Pin-Figeac, la Tour
Figeac, Troplong-Mondot, Villemaurine and
Yon-Figeac.

CHÂTEAU LE PIN, POMEROL
The story behind this wine is almost unbelievable. The first vintage of Le Pin was created in 1979; by 1982, it was being traded at £30,000 a case (12 bottles), making it one of the most expensive wines ever. This remarkable achievement is down to Jacques Thienpont, a member of the Belgian family who own the Vieux Château Certan property among others, who spotted the potential of the terroir of a tiny parcel of land that came up for sale. Apart from its stellar quality, the wine fetches high prices because only 6000 bottles of it are made each year – the estate owns just 2 ha (5 acres) of vineyards. Le Pin was one of the first of a growing number of wines that are described as 'garage' wines, so called because the wine is produced in non-conventional settings – the first vintage of Le Pin, for example, was made in a concrete shack. Even today, Thienpont uses no machinery in the winery – he does things his own way and likes to make the wine as simply as possible. Created from 100 per cent Merlot, the wine is aged in new oak barrels for 12 to 18 months to give a magical, velvety wine, rich in the aromas of raspberries and cherries, that is almost Burgundian in character. Once tasted, never forgotten.

Literally across a country lane from Château Cheval Blanc, St-Emilion suddenly ends to become the appellation of Pomerol. With just 832 ha (2056 acres) under vine, this is the smallest of Bordeaux's principal appellations and has a long history of not really being noticed – its wines were relatively unknown outside France and the Benelux countries until the 1960s. Today, and now that the rest of the world has caught on to its charms, it is responsible for producing two of world's most stratospherically expensive, cult wines: Château Pétrus and Château Le Pin. These represent the pinnacle of the Pomerol style – an intriguing perfume of truffles and mint, and rich, smooth, almost creamy flavours of plums, as well as raisins, chocolate and roasted nuts.

Pomerol is located on a gently sloping plateau with soils that are based on a deep layer of clay – and clay is what the Merlot grape variety adores best of all. Many Pomerol wines are made up of almost 100 per cent of it, which is what makes them so very different from other Bordeaux reds. By the way, both Pomerol and the St-Emilion appellations apply to red wines only, that is, you will never see a bottle of white wine labelled either St-Emilion or Pomerol.

If the prices of St-Emilion and Pomerol wines have set you reeling (and they may well do when you see them), then consider buying the red wines of Lalande-de-Pomerol, which is a good Pomerol lookalike, Côtes de Castillon, or Bordeaux-Côtes de Francs (most especially Château Puygueraud). The latter appellation has the warmest and driest climate in Bordeaux, so its potential is enormous. Alternatively, travel further west to the hilly Fronsac and Canon-Fronsac area. These produce some firm and rich, Merlot-dominated red wines that offer good value for money. In theory, there ought to be a difference between the two because the vineyards of Canon-Fronsac, which lie at the heart of the Fronsac region, are south-facing (and therefore catch more sunshine) and are planted on better soils. In practice, though, there is little to separate the two wines.

BORDEAUX

Southeast of the city

**CLASSIFIED WINES
OF THE GRAVES**
Bouscaut, Carbonnieux,
Domaine de Chevalier,
Couhins, Couhins-Lurton,
Fieuzal, Haut-Bailly, Haut-
Brion, Latour Martillac,
Laville Haut-Brion,
Malartic-Lagravière,
la Mission Haut-Brion,
d'Olivier, Pape Clément,
Smith-Haut-Lafitte and
la Tour Haut-Brion.

From the suburbs of the city of Bordeaux right down to the south of Langon lies the sub-region of Graves, which contains the appellations of Graves and Pessac-Léognan. Originally, Pessac-Léognan was part of the Graves appellation, but it declared independence and claimed its own appellation contrôlée in 1987. Unfortunately, all 16 of the Crus Classés of Graves (including all of Bordeaux's dry white Crus Classés) are now located in the Pessac-Léognan appellation. In other words, while the Crus Classés are still officially called Crus Classés de Graves, what you see on the label is Pessac-Léognan.

Graves is called Graves because it is the French word for 'gravel', although, once again, most of the gravelly soil is found in Pessac-Léognan and it is here that the bulk of the Cabernet Sauvignon-led, mellow, plummy and blackcurranty red wines are made, and they're very good too. Indeed, this is home to the only Bordeaux red wine outside the Médoc to be awarded Premier Grand Cru Classé status in the 1855 classification: Château Haut-Brion.

While the Graves appellation produces almost equal quantities of red and white wine, its reputation has been founded upon its dry whites, which are either snappy and fresh or soft-centred and nutty edged (the latter fermented and aged in oak barrels).

TASTING NOTES
Clos Floridène, Graves Blanc, Denis Dubourdieu, 2001
Oz says: Good. Full-bodied, savoury, deep and ripe, with flavours of biscuit, custard and nectarines.
James says: This is super. I really like it. There are all sorts of riotously exciting, fresh, crisp fruits. It's all bubble gum and ocean wind nonsense. It sort of makes you want an ice cream because there's a hint of vanilla in it. It's fantastic.

Bordeaux's gorgeous sweet white wines

Bordeaux is also famed for its superb, luscious, sweet wines – most notably Sauternes and Barsac, arguably the best sweet wines in the world – which are made from a blend of Sémillon, Sauvignon Blanc and Muscadelle grape varieties.

The vineyards of the villages of Sauternes and Barsac hug the Ciron river, a tiny tributary of the Garonne, just north of the town of Langon. The grapes bathe in the humid mists that rise from the river each day during the autumn, caused by the cold waters of the Ciron colliding with the warmer waters of the Garonne. It is these mists that encourage 'noble rot' (see page 56), a prerequisite for all great sweet wine.

Barsac is actually the largest of the five communes in Sauternes and, perhaps a little confusingly, can therefore be labelled Barsac, Sauternes or even Sauternes-Barsac – as long as it is a sweet wine, that is, because the dry whites can only be called Bordeaux Blanc (why, oh why, does everything have to be so complicated in France?). As a rule, Barsac is slightly less sticky than Sauternes, yet they still cost a bundle, especially the Crus Classés.

Prices can go through the roof for these memorable, long-lived wines, partly because they cannot necessarily be made every year (sometimes, the natural conditions don't favour the correct type of rot). If you can't afford to buy even a half-bottle, do make a point of tasting it while you're in the area. You'll relish every drop of this voluptuous, syrupy-sweet nectar, which exudes a cornucopia of flavours – honey, orange marmalade, barley sugar, green apples, beeswax, dried fruits, pineapple, peaches, quince, coconut, tropical fruit, butterscotch and marzipan – balanced by a zingy spine of acidity that stops the wine from becoming too cloying.

Cadillac, Cérons, Loupiac and Ste-Croix-du-Mont also make sweet wines, but they are lighter in body and never as complex as Sauternes and Barsac. On the other hand, they are far more affordable.

The people of Bordeaux often serve Sauternes and Barsac as an aperitif, icy cold. But, perhaps surprisingly, it's also lip-smackingly delicious with pâté de foie gras de canard (duck-liver pâté) – in spite of the sweetness of the wine, its high acidity cuts through the richness of the pâté. You should also try foie gras de canard à la Bordelaise, a hot dish of foie gras that is baked for 20 minutes, the fat is drained off and then it's baked for a further ten minutes. This is usually served with peeled, unripe grapes that have been marinated in Cognac.

If you want to take some foie gras home, you can buy it very easily from one of the many markets in the city of Bordeaux. Two of the best are the Sunday market, Marché des Quais, held on the historic Quai des Chartrons (the cradle of the Bordeaux wine trade) on the banks of the river Garonne, and the Marché Capucins, known as the 'belly of Bordeaux', which has been held for over 300 years. As well as foie gras, you could also buy confit de canard (a rather special duck pâté), Arcachon oysters and Gironde caviare. For the sweet-toothed, buy St-Emilion macaroons, which are tiny, round, crunchy cakes that melt in your mouth when you bite into them, invented in 1519 by the nuns at the Annonciades convent. It's also great fun to go to the Saturday morning Marché Royal, which spreads around the St-Michel church and sells everything from live animals to Middle Eastern music. The tourist office (see page 217) can furnish you with a map and directions to find all these markets easily.

TASTING NOTES
Château Climens, Barsac, 1997
Oz says: Full, round and soft, with gentle flavours of nuts, barley sugar, ripe peach and the rich syrup of pineapple. There's also a deep layer of fat lanolin and beeswax. Strangely, it's not intensely sweet.
James says: Whoa. Far too sweet for me.

THE 1855 SAUTERNES CLASSIFICATION
PREMIER CRU SUPÉRIEUR:
d'Yquem (Sauternes).
PREMIERS CRUS:
Climens (Barsac), Clos Haut-Peyraguey
(Sauternes), Coutet (Barsac), Guiraud (Sauternes),
Lafaurie-Peyraguey (Sauternes), Rabaud-
Promis (Sauternes), Rayne-Vigneau (Sauternes),
Rieussec (Sauternes), Sigalas-Rabaud
(Sauternes), Suduirat (Sauternes) and la
Tour-Blanche (Sauternes).
DEUXIÈMES CRUS:
d'Arche (Sauternes), Broustet (Barsac),
Caillou (Barsac), Doisy-Daëne (Barsac),
Doisy-Dubroca (Barsac), Doisy-Védrines
(Barsac), Filhot (Sauternes), Lamothe-Despujols
(Sauternes), Lamothe-Guignard (Sauternes),
de Malle (Sauternes), de Myrat (Sauternes),
Nairac (Barsac), Romer-du-Hayot (Sauternes)
and Suau (Barsac).

**CHÂTEAU D'YQUEM, PREMIER GRAND CRU
CLASSÉ, SAUTERNES**
Back in 1855 when the people of Bordeaux were
busy classifying their châteaux, the powers-that-
be put Château d'Yquem very firmly at the top of the
list. They considered the glorious, sweet Sauternes
that it produces the very finest wine of Bordeaux
and the most expensive – and nothing has changed
since. Even today, many people consider this wine
to be the greatest wine of Bordeaux.

Production is not large (around 95,000 bottles
a year), even though the vineyard holding is pretty
large (103 ha/255 acres). Château d'Yquem
ferments the grape juice in new oak barrels and
the wine is then left to age in them for three and
a half years before bottling. This in itself means
that up to 20 per cent of each vintage of Yquem
is lost through evaporation ('the angels' share',
as it is often described).

Such a small annual production coupled with
a constant demand for the wine leads, inevitably,
to rocket-high prices, especially given the fact that
it isn't released at all in some years (if the wine
isn't up to scratch, it isn't labelled Yquem) – indeed,
it's one of the world's most expensive wines.

Yquem is now owned by LVMH (shorthand for
the Louis Vuitton Moët Hennessy group) and, like
Château Pichon-Longueville, throws up yet another
example of international commerce tapping into
the top end of the wine industry. But then, LVMH
(in turn, part-owned by Christian Dior) is the
world's largest luxury-goods conglomerate owning
a large number of prestigious brands – top wine
names include Krug, Moët & Chandon, Ruinart,
Mercier and Veuve Clicquot champagnes, and then
there's TAG Heuer watches, Givenchy perfumes
and the Donna Karan, Kenzo and Thomas Pink
fashion labels, to name but a few.

The making of botrytized wines It sounds unlikely, and it may seem faintly repugnant, but the world's greatest sweet wines can only be made from ultra-ripe grapes that have literally rotted on the vine. And, yes, we are talking about mouldy, furry grapes here. Mind you, it has to be exactly the right type of rot ('pourriture noble', or 'noble rot' – in other words, not grey rot, black rot or sour rot) induced by exactly the right type of fungus, namely *Botrytis cinerea* (hence the phrase botrytized wines).

As the grapes become infected and the skins start to weaken because of the rot, the water inside the grapes is slowly sucked out by the warm, autumnal air, causing them to shrivel and shrink to a shadow of their former size – and they go mouldy. Unfortunately, this doesn't necessarily happen to all the bunches at the same time and so the grapes have to be picked bunch by bunch and sometimes grape by grape. The pickers very often have to go through the vines time after time (at Château d'Yquem, for example, they can do this 11 times). This labour-intensive task is one reason for the high price of the wine. Equally critical, though, is that when the time comes for the grapes to be pressed, they yield only minute quantities of intensely concentrated juice. To put this into some kind of perspective, the grapes of one vine normally supply enough juice to make a bottle of wine; here in Sauternes, a single vine may produce only a glass of wine.

The juice is so high in natural sugar and acidity that the yeasts cannot work efficiently. In fact, a stage is reached when the yeasts just give up and die. It is the unfermented sugar left behind that gives the wine its glorious, mouth-coating sweetness and richness. And, no, you cannot taste the mould that caused this incredible transformation from rotting grapes to fabulous wine.

The best of the rest

On the right bank of the Gironde river, the Côtes de Blaye appellation covers white wines only and most of these are dry to taste. You may end up in the town of Blaye itself if you are planning to cross the Gironde on the car ferry that runs between Blaye and Lamarque – and there's also the remains of a seventeenth-century citadel to look at, occupying a prime position on a rocky outcrop overlooking the whole of the estuary. While here, you might want to try a red Premières Côtes de Blaye. Until recently, these were very jammy and sweet, but a new generation of winemakers is making much fresher and drier styles – try the Merlot. Top wines come under the Blaye appellation.

Upstream of Blaye is the hilly Côtes de Bourg, one of Bordeaux's forgotten areas (good news for the wallet), which is such a shame because it has everything going for it – sloping vineyards to catch the sun, a slightly warmer climate than other parts of Bordeaux that helps to keep spring frosts at bay and enough gravel in the soils to suit Cabernet Sauvignon (though Merlot dominates). Try the red wines for their appealing, earthy, blackcurranty flavours.

If you've been missing the thrill of steep slopes, then drive along the meandering 60-km (38-mile) stretch of the right bank of the Garonne river that forms the Premières Côtes de Bordeaux sub-region where the land tumbles from a limestone escarpment right down to the river. In fact, this is perhaps the prettiest part of Bordeaux. But is it worth stopping to buy the local wine (labelled Premières Côtes de Bordeaux)? Well, the area is known for its sweet wines – the communes of Cadillac, Loupiac and St-Croix-du-Mont are located here – but if you don't have a sweet tooth, sample the tasty, juicy, fruity red wines instead. Some of Bordeaux's most pleasant rosé wines are made here as well.

The sub-region of Entre-Deux-Mers, as mentioned previously, is well known for its crisp, grassy, appley, dry white wines (its red wines can only ever be labelled as simple Bordeaux Rouge because the Entre-Deux-Mers appellation is only for white wines). Some producers – and most of these are co-operatives who make about 12 million bottles each year – age their white wine in new oak barrels, which adds a delicious creaminess alongside hints of apricot, but oaked or unoaked, these are terrific everyday guzzlers that won't break the bank.

Entre-Deux-Mers is also the engine room of Bordeaux because this is where 75 per cent of generic Bordeaux Blanc and Rouge is made. In turn, 75 per cent of Bordeaux Rouge is used for own-label supermarket wines, as well as brands such as Mouton Cadet. You can sip these while visiting one of the fortified, walled towns called bastides, built in the thirteenth and fourteenth centuries by the English and French rulers to mark out their respective territories – Créon and Sauveterre-de-Guyenne are particularly fine examples.

CHÂTEAU BAUDUC, CRÉON

When entrepreneurial, down-to-earth Englishman Gavin Quinney decided that he wanted to set up an internet wine business, he took himself off on a fact-finding tour of the world. To say that it was whirlwind is something of an understatement – for example, he visited no fewer than 250 Australian wineries in just six weeks. Eventually, he pitched up in Bordeaux where he fell instantly in love with Château Bauduc, a beautiful nineteenth-century stone building, complete with twin turrets and colonnades, and decided to buy it there and then, without even consulting his wife, Angela. (You can just imagine the phone call: 'Darling, I've just bought a château in France ...').

The family upped sticks and moved into the property in 1999. At that time, the estate was churning out grapes for cheap table wine (real plonk, in other words), so Quinney immediately set about improving the vineyard, ploughing £30,000 into it before he had even blinked, which supports the old winemakers' adage that the only way to make a small fortune in wine is to start with a big one. From Quinney's first vintage, there has been much acclaim for Château Bauduc's very affordable red, white and rosé wines.

Breaking with every tradition in the Bordeaux wine trade, the wines are sold direct to consumers in the UK (though if you're visiting the area, you can also buy them at the estate). Given that it's often a very tough job to sell Bordeaux Blanc, Rouge and Rosé, especially in the UK where French wine sales are falling steadily in the face of fierce competition from countries such as Australia and California, Quinney's achievements in such a short space of time are quite remarkable.

LOOK FOR:

▸ Château Bauduc Bordeaux Supérieur Rouge (a blend of 70 per cent Merlot/30 per cent Cabernet Sauvignon)

▸ Clos des Quinze Premières Côtes de Bordeaux (an oak-aged red blend of Merlot, Cabernet Sauvignon and Cabernet Franc)

▸ Château Bauduc Bordeaux Rosé (a very gluggable, fruity and dry style)

▸ Château Bauduc Bordeaux Blanc Sec (a deliciously crisp and zingy dry white made mainly from Sauvignon Blanc)

▸ Les Trois Hectares (an aromatic, complex, oak-aged white wine made in limited quantities solely from the fruit of 59-year-old Sémillon vines)

Finally, it's worth driving down the Dordogne valley to the little town of Castillon-la-Bataille, east of Libourne, because it played a very significant role in the history of Aquitaine. This was where the final battle was fought among the French, the Bretons and the English that marked the end of the Hundred Years War in 1453. The English lost the battle, lost Aquitaine and, of course, lost the vineyards and wine that went with it. The town is also the centre of the Côtes de Castillon commune that offers winning, blackcurrenty and minty red wines, the best coming from the slopes of the limestone plateau that is shared with St-Emilion.

LES SOURCES DE CAUDALIE, CHÂTEAU SMITH HAUT-LAFITTE, BORDEAUX-MARTILLAC
This upmarket spa centred in the heart of the Château Smith Haut-Lafitte vineyards offers a unique course of 'vinothérapie' (vine therapy) treatments that combine the virtues of naturally warm, thermal-spring waters with products of the vine. These include red-wine baths, Merlot wraps, crushed Cabernet Sauvignon scrubs and massages with grape-pip oil, all washed down with red-vine-leaf tea. Well, they do say that wine is good for you.

A WORD OF WARNING
Not all Bordeaux wine is good. For every great wine, there are hundreds of downright dire examples, so it's important to choose the best producers from the top vintages. This will mean forking out a Henry II-size ransom in some cases, but there are reasonably priced wines. If you go for the very cheapest wines, well, frankly, you could be getting better value and better flavours elsewhere.

WHEN TO DRINK THE WINES OF BORDEAUX
▸ The red wines of Premières Cotes de Bordeaux and Premières Cotes de Blaye can be stashed away for two to three years from the vintage date
▸ Basic St-Emilion, Moulis, Lalande-de-Pomerol and Fronsac are ready within three to five years, but many demand more time
▸ Côtes de Bourg will keep for six to ten years
▸ Top dry whites (such as white Graves and white Pessac-Léognan) can develop for up to eight years Margaux and red Pessac-Léognan matures at seven to 12 years
▸ Top reds Canon-Fronsac, Pomerol, Pauillac, St-Julien, St-Estèphe and St-Emilion Grand Crus Classés will age for a minimum of ten years Sauternes and Barsac can be drunk young, but will age for 20 years at least. Other sweeter Bordeaux whites should be drunk young

Food and wine matching

The versatile claret is exceptionally tasty with an array of roasts –
partridge, beef, pheasant, chicken, goose, pigeon, duck, pork, lamb
and turkey. It also partners lamb-based recipes such as Irish stew,
shepherd's pie and kebabs, as well as pork or beef casseroles, fried
steak, beef Wellington and steak and kidney pudding. The locals drink
it with Gouda cheese. For the ultimate match, choose a mature,
classic Haut-Médoc.

The restrained style of Bordeaux whites means that they can be
drunk alongside a wide variety of dishes. Looking at starters and snacks,
try it with asparagus soup, French onion soup, tomato soup, seafood
chowder, asparagus with hollandaise sauce, mussels, grilled prawns,
whitebait, crab, Caesar salad, avocado with prawns and goat's cheese
tart. Turning to main courses, the crunchy acidity of white Graves works
especially well with any fish recipe that involves a rich, creamy sauce.
The creamy nuttiness of Pessac-Léognan is good with chunky fish
such as halibut, monkfish or cod.

When it comes to puddings, the sweeter, stickier and more complex
the dessert, the less likely it is to do a wine any favours. Normally I
would partner Sauternes with simple fruit desserts or drink on its own.
However, it does go very well with cheese – it's wonderful with Cheshire
and Roquefort in particular. Meanwhile, strong hard cheeses such as
Cheddar, Caerphilly and old Gouda make even the toughest red wine
seem soft.

Bordeaux by James

If you are planning an educational wine tour of France, Bordeaux is an especially good place to start. Bordeaux alone is enough to convince you that French wine is far too complex a subject to tackle in one lifetime, and that will free up the rest of your holiday to enjoy all the other things France has to offer: castles, scenery, beaches, lovely D roads, cafes, bebefoot with the locals – the list is almost infinite.

Any bottle of Bordeaux wine will serve to make the point. What is it, exactly? No label will proclaim, 'This is a nice bottle of Bordeaux,' because this is France, where making things more complex than they need to be is a national trait. Local politics, geography and wanton obfuscation play as big a part as grape-growing in the French wine business. This sort of thing is known as manigance – a combination of hanky-panky, jiggery-pokery, and skullduggery.

The label won't reveal, for example, which grapes are used in the wine. You're supposed to know that a Bordeaux red will be made largely with the cabernet and merlot varieties. In the new world they'd print this information in large letters, but not in France, because then you'd know and that wouldn't do at all. Single château stuff is generally considered good, especially if it's bottled on the premises, but even then you can't be certain. If you make it all the way to Château-neuf-du-Pape in the Rhône you will discover that it isn't actually a château at all, but a whole village. A wine might also be vin de pays – 'country wine' – which means it doesn't satisfy the requirements of the appellation committee. But this isn't necessarily reason for despair. True, it could be filthy grog produced by a faux-communist co-operative and suitable only for re-distillation into biofuel, but it could be the work of a wine anarchist who wants to stray outside of the established rules in order to make something more exciting. And sometimes they succeed. But how will you know?

And this is before we consider the vintage, how the wine has been aged, and how it has been stored. In essence – and this is a bloody convoluted essence – unless you are familiar with a particular producer and know your good years, you can't be sure of anything.

But there is a solution. Make friends with Oz Clarke, ask him to introduce you to his aristocratic château-dwelling chums, and thank the Good Lord for the Scarlet Pimpernel. Some of this stuff is truly fantastic, with woody high notes etc. etc. etc. But it's expensive: £60 for a single bottle is not unusual.

Sadly, Oz Clarke won't allow me to print his phone number, so you might find yourself alone in a cave or supermarket with just a tenner to spend.

And now you're stuffed.

CHAPTER 2 LANGUEDOC-ROUSSILLON

CÉVENNES

PIC SAINT LOUP

Avignon

Nîmes

CÔTEAUX DU LANGUEDOC

COSTIÈRES DU NÎMES

Minerve

Faugères

R. Orb

R. Hérault

N110

Petit Rhône

R. Rhône

MINERVOIS

Montpellier

Lunel

St Jean de minervois

St Chinian

Béziers

A9 AUTOROUTE

Canal du Midi

Sète

Rhône Delta

Carcassonne

R. Aude

Narbonne

Pinet

Cap d'Agde

MEDITERRANEAN SEA

Limoux

CORBIÈRES

Rivesaltes

Perpignan

R. Agly

Collioure
Banyuls

The swathe of vines carpeting the vast tract of land that arcs around the rim of the Mediterranean coastline from the Spanish border to the Rhône delta forms the region of Languedoc-Roussillon. It is the largest grape-growing area in the world with some 160,000 ha (400,000 acres) of vines – one-third of all French land under vine – which produces over two billion bottles of wine each year (a staggering 25 per cent of all French wines). Red wines, by far the best of the region, account for nearly 90 per cent of production.

It may be France's biggest wine region, but it has never been its best in terms of quality. Indeed, 30-odd years ago, Languedoc-Roussillon was characterized by its very cheap and rough wines that were poured into nameless blends of Vin de Table or 'table wine' (the most basic of French wine: see page 21) or simply turned into industrial alcohol, which was often more profitable for the growers. Today, however, it yields many of the country's most exhilarating, tasty and affordable wines, and the sheer rate of progress that has taken place so far has been nothing short of astonishing.

So what prompted the move towards producing wines of better quality? Well, the French themselves have slowly been consuming less and less wine each year. In the 1950s, each person was drinking 170 litres (45 gal.) of wine each year; by 2002, the annual consumption per head had dropped to just 56 litres (12.3 gal.). A declining market at home also coincided with the first stirrings from the awakening New World winemaking countries such as Australia and the USA that went on to steal a fair wodge of France's important export market (especially in the UK). No-one wanted the wines of Languedoc-Roussillon any more.

With the advent of European Union subsidies, however, good incentives were provided to encourage improvement in the vineyards and to help pay for the introduction of state-of-the-art winemaking equipment in the wineries. The region was reorganized and the Vin de Pays ('country wine' – see page 21) category was set up to provide a regional identity – only 70,000 ha (173,000 acres) of Languedoc-Roussillon produce appellation-contrôlée wine – which heralded the arrival of a new breed of visionary winemaker who has not been afraid to experiment with the so-called international grape varieties (Chardonnay, Cabernet Sauvignon, Syrah et al.). These are not generally permitted to be grown under Languedoc-Roussillon appellation-contrôlée laws, but they are allowed to be planted under the more flexible and less stringent Vin de Pays rules. But this is not to overlook the massive improvements that have also been made to the traditional appellation-contrôlée wines over the past 30 years and these are now beginning to win the accolades that so many of them deserve. The majority of these wines are made from a blend of grape varieties (any of Carignan, Cinsaut, Grenache, Mourvèdre, Syrah and, sometimes, Cabernet Sauvignon for reds and rosés. The traditional white wines are created primarily from Grenache Blanc, Clairette and Bourbulenc, with growing amounts of Marsanne, Roussanne and Rolle, the local name for the Vermentino grape variety).

In general, the climate is Mediterranean, with plenty of sun (the region enjoys 300 days of sunshine each year), mild, rainy winters, moderate springs and autumns, and hot, dry summers. In fact, after Corsica, this region is the hottest in France and summertime temperatures frequently reach 30°C (86°F) – though, in 2001, Nîmes recorded a temperature of 43°C (110°F). Everywhere is very windy, which helps to cool things down, though the coastline, sheltered by the mountains, tends to be warmer and than inland areas, even with its sea breezes. The temperature falls as the land rises to form the mountains whose valleys tend to be a little damper; neighbouring valleys very often have different weather patterns: one wet, the next dry and sunny. The downside to the climate is the extremes of weather that can sometimes occur. For example, spectacular hailstorms that can strip a car of its paint; in September 2002, 68.6 cm (27 in.) of rain fell in one day, causing extensive flooding.

69

Stainless steel is the preferred material nowadays for fermenting and storing wine. If the owner of this vat recognises it's his, he might want to turn the tap off and stop adding to the European wine lake.

With the Pyrénées, the Cévennes, the Montagne Noire and the Massif Central as a backdrop to its Mediterranean coastline, the landscape of the Languedoc-Roussillon varies greatly, but much of it is occupied by the 'garrigue', a wild, sparsely populated, arid and rocky limestone plateau covered in dwarf trees, bay, thyme, fennel, rosemary, mint and lavender.

As you begin to drive around the region, you will see numerous signs reading 'Dégustation', which indicates that a free tasting is available. You can stop and taste the wines at these places, and if you like what you taste you can buy direct from the producer, sometimes at a significant discount compared with shop prices.

Key traditional southern red-grape varieties

Carignan is the most widely planted grape variety in Languedoc-Roussillon. It's very tolerant of heat, drought and wind, so it's perfectly suited to the prevailing climate. It provides colour, alcohol and tannin, and if the wine is made by the carbonic-maceration method (see page 202), it can also add plenty of fruit flavours to the blend.

Cinsaut is also another grape variety that stands up well to intense heat. It makes unexciting wines that are often blended with Carignan to balance the high levels of tannin. It's often at its best in pale rosés.

Grenache performs well here, giving powerful wines rich in the flavours of soft red fruits, white pepper and, sometimes, hints of tobacco, chocolate, coffee and, believe it or not, stones.

Mourvèdre is one of the hardest grapes to ripen, so it adds a lot of tannin to the blend alongside aromas and flavours of black fruits, black pepper, spice and herbs.

Syrah (aka Shiraz) grown here offers a roasted, smoky character, a host of dark fruit and spice flavours, sometimes a violet scent as well as hints of mushrooms, tar and burnt rubber. It, too, adds plenty of colour and tannin to the blend.

Key traditional southern white-grape varieties

Clairette can provide a slightly musky aroma and an apple flavour to the blend as long as the grape yields are kept low. Otherwise, it is a very dull grape variety.

Macabeo is another very neutral white-grape variety in that it doesn't deliver much flavour. But it enjoys the southern heat and contributes body to the blend.

Rolle is highly aromatic and therefore provides perfume to the blend, as well as acidity.

Marsanne is a vigorous vine, but as long as its yield of grapes is kept under control it can contribute a honeysuckle aroma and, sometimes, a flavour of fresh peaches.

Roussanne hates the wind and is a late-ripening variety, so it's quite difficult to cultivate. But it can add a gentle herbiness and hints of honey, apricot and flowers to southern white blends.

Viognier is increasingly used for its rich apricot fruit and floral scent.

Vin de Pays

Vin de Pays ('country wine') is hugely important in this part of France – over 80 per cent of all the country's Vins de Pays comes from here. The system was set up to provide a regional identity, but it also allows producers to break free of the chains attached to appellation-contrôlée wines. For example, it gives them the ability to plant non-traditional grape varieties in places where the grower thinks they will make better wines than the traditional varieties would do and, without being too cynical, wines that are likely to sell more readily. Slap 'Chardonnay' on a label, say, and the wine is more likely to be snapped up by consumers than a wine labelled with some obscure place name.

Vin de Pays ought to be a designation that is effortless to understand and to a great extent it is, chiefly because the name of the grape variety from which the wine has been made is printed on the label. But the French never make life easy. There are three separate levels even within the Vin de Pays classification.

Firstly, there are regional Vins de Pays enveloping a group of geographical departments. The umbrella Vin de Pays d'Oc covers the whole of the Languedoc-Roussillon region and is the most important regional Vin de Pays producing 530 million bottles a year. It accounts for 70 per cent of total Vin de Pays exports and is the primary source of French varietal wines (those made from a single grape variety only). Then there are the departmental Vins de Pays for each individual department within each region – in Languedoc-Roussillon these are Vin de Pays des Pyrénées-Orientales, Vin de Pays de l'Aude, Vin de Pays de l'Hérault and Vin de Pays du Gard. Last but not least are the more precise zonal Vins de Pays that apply to local districts – for example, Vin de Pays des Côtes de Thongue in the Hérault department. There are 55 zonal Vins de Pays in Languedoc-Roussillon in total. Here's three to watch out for:

▸ Vin de Pays de Caux in the Hérault department (for red wines, especially those made from the Carignan grape variety)

▸ Vin de Pays de Hauterive en Pays d'Aude (for white wines, especially those made from the Viognier grape variety)

▸ Vin de Pays des Côtes de Thongue in the Hérault department

Cabardès and Côtes de Malepère

Starting in the west of the region just north of the dramatic, walled, medieval town of Carcassonne and lying to the southeast of Gaillac, the cool, upland Cabardès and Côtes de la Malepère appellations – separated only by the historic Canal du Midi – produce perfumed, mouth-filling red wines that are well worth trying. These rising stars (often sold at bargain prices) offer two styles depending on the precise mix of grape varieties used in the blend: a high percentage of Grenache gives warm, juicy, strawberry-flecked wines, while those that contain a large amount of Cabernet Sauvignon or Cabernet Franc boast blackcurranty flavours.

Limoux

An hour's drive south of Carcassonne, down the Aude river valley, brings you to the town of Limoux and its wines. Set at the foot of the Pyrénées and with a distinctly cooler climate than other Languedoc-Roussillon areas, this was the first appellation in Languedoc-Roussillon that was allowed to grow the white Chardonnay and Chenin Blanc grape varieties and, furthermore, local winemaking laws state that the wines must be fermented in oak barrels – which adds extra flavour. Indeed, the white wines of Limoux are among the best of the region. There is also red wine that must be made from at least 50 per cent of the Merlot grape variety.

Limoux is equally well known for Blanquette de Limoux – thought to be the oldest sparkling wine in the world and dating back to at least 1388 – and Crémant de Limoux, both excellent traditional-method sparkling wines. Generally speaking, good fizz can only be made from grapes that possess high levels of natural acidity, which is hard to achieve in the sun-baked Languedoc-Roussillon region. In the hilly Limoux, however, the heat is moderated by the influence of the Atlantic ocean, especially on the higher slopes of the valleys where the air is cooler. The difference between the two wines is that Blanquette de Limoux is made mostly

RESTAURANT

from the Mauzac grape variety, which gives a sharp, green-apple flavour, whereas the Crémant contains a high percentage of Chardonnay (alongside Mauzac, Chenin Blanc and Pinot Noir) and is therefore softer and more complex in personality. There is also a small amount of rustic Blanquette Méthode Ancestrale (see page 121). Around 80 per cent of Limoux wines are produced by the modern and progressive Sieur d'Arques co-operative (the co-operatives still account for 70 per cent of all Languedoc-Roussillon wines).

Crémant de Limoux is the perfect partner to pebradous, which are biscuits smeared with a pepper-flavoured paste. Another tasty local speciality is dried, salted, pig's liver, marinated in oil before being sautéed and served with paper-thin slices of artichoke. There's also Limoux pork fricassee, which was traditionally served on the farms at slaughter time. The pork is cooked in a thick, white sauce and the dish is usually served with beans. By the way, if you're staying in this area over a weekend, it's worth going to the Sunday morning food market in Espéraza, about 32 km (20 miles) to the south of Limoux.

Lunch is a constant obstacle in the French working day and can last up to three hours. It got in the way of our filming, and certainly got in the way of the local signwriter.

LANGUEDOC-ROUSSILLON

75

Corbières and Fitou

If you're heading for the city of Narbonne on the Mediterranean coast from Limoux, you may choose to backtrack to the Canal du Midi and then turn east until Perpignan, and then head south. This will take you through the Corbières district, an enormous, wild, dramatic, mountainous area with over 15,000 ha (37,050 acres) under vine. Given its size, it's not surprising that wine styles vary depending on precisely where in the district the grapes are grown. In fact, there are 11 sub-zones that reflect the differences in the landscape and climate, the top wines hailing from the sub-zones of Boutenac, Lagrasse and Durban. Corbières is home to some of best red wines in Languedoc-Roussillon, full of the flavours of juicy dark fruits and aromas of spice, sun-baked earth and the wild herbs that pepper the hillsides. These are just the kind of wines that go well with the local guinea fowl and partridge.

Given where it is made, it's not surprising that the red wines of Fitou share the same kind of flavours as Corbières. It is produced in two zones within Corbières: Fitou Maritime, near Etang de Leucate on the coast, and Fitou Montagneux, located inland where the vines clamber up to 300 metres (984 ft) on the slopes of the craggy hills. These mountain wines are the best by a long way, so do make a point of tasting them, either those made by the local Tuchan co-operative, or single estate wines.

CHÂTEAU DE LASTOURS

This is an incredible place. It is one of the biggest and one of the best estates in Corbières, creating delicious red, white and rosé wines from 130 ha (321 acres) of vines located on stony ground some 300 metres (1000 ft) above sea level. But this isn't why it is incredible. It's incredible because, apart from bringing in some extra help at the time of the grape harvest, all of the 60 people who work there have a mental health illness – Château de Lastours is a charitable institution that offers the work direction to enable this.

Jean-Marie Lignères, who runs the estate, is a qualified winemaker, but he has other passions. For a start, he has allowed an experimental, seven-turbine wind-farm to be constructed on top of the mountains, which has become a noted feature of the local landscape, visible for miles around. He has also designed an exciting, four-wheel-drive track through 700 ha (2093 acres) of the estate that is used as a training ground for the Paris–Dakar Rally.

LOOK FOR:

▶ Cuvée Simone Descamps, the top label of the range, named after the founder of the institution
▶ The red Château de Lastours, a concentrated wine made from a blend of Grenache and Carignan grape varieties grown on land nearest to the sea
▶ La Grande Rompue, which is more savoury and herbal in character
▶ Arnaud de Berre, an easy-drinking red wine
▶ Chatellénie, another light-bodied red wine

CHÂTEAU L'HOSPITALET, LA CLAPE

In 1995, and after many years of searching for just the right property, Gérard Bertrand, a former professional rugby player and son of a Corbières winemaker, bought an estate called Château l'Hospitalet, situated in the La Clape area in 52 ha (128 acres) of land conquered from the rockiest part of the garrigue scrubland overhanging the Mediterranean sea. Here, he grows 15 different grape varieties, including all of the principal traditional varieties, plus Chardonnay, Viognier, Sauvignon Blanc, Cabernet Sauvignon and Merlot.

The winery is huge and contains every bit of modern winemaking equipment going. The subterranean cellar in which the wines are matured was hollowed out of the unforgiving rock 10 metres (33 ft) below ground.

Apart from the red and white wines of Château l'Hospitalet, Gérard Bertrand's range includes red wines from Domaine de Villemajou in Corbières (his old family home and the oldest-known winemaking 'domaine' – one of the French terms used to describe a winemaking estate – in Corbières), the red wines of Château Laville Bertrou in Minervois (acquired in 1997) and the red and white H de l'Hospitalet and Domaine Cigalus, both of which are top-quality Vins de Pays. He is as creative as possible in the way the wines are marketed and has a strong commitment to branding.

Unusually, wine tourism is at the heart of this estate's activities. Its hotel, restaurant, bistro, museum, art gallery and music festivals are some of its attractions.

LOOK FOR:

▶ Extrème (red)
▶ Summum (red and white)
▶ Cigalus Vin de Pays d'Oc
▶ Minervois Les Matins d'Aurore

Banyuls and Collioure

If you don't want to backtrack from Limoux, you could choose to drive the Route des Pyrénées to join the Mediterranean coast at the attractive fishing village of Collioure. Here, the pretty coastal vineyards that rub shoulders with Spain climb away from the sea into the foothills of the Albères mountains. Red, white and rosé Collioure is made, but the district is best known for Banyuls, France's finest Vin Doux Naturel (see page 122). Grenache, the principal grape variety of this wine, thrives in the sunny, schistose, steeply terraced vineyards held in place by nothing else but dry-stone walls.

It's worthwhile knowing what all the different labels mean. Vintage Banyuls, often labelled Rimage, is bottled at six to 12 months after harvest to give a port-like style that tastes of raisins and plums. The richer Banyuls Grand Cru indicates that the wine has been made from at least 75 per cent of Grenache and that it has been aged in oak barrels for at least 30 months. Rancio means that the wine has been deliberately exposed to air in order to oxidize it and the resultant wine tastes very similar to Madeira.

Before you leave the area, try any dish that is described on menus as à la Collioure: these are served with a local sauce of anchovy and garlic-flavoured mayonnaise – Collioure is famous for its anchovies, which are still processed by hand by the 'anchoïeurs'. Mind you, finding a wine that goes with them is something of a challenge.

DOMAINE PIÉTRI-GÉRAUD, COLLIOURE

This 14-ha (35-acre) estate, which has been in the Piétri-Géraud family for generations, is run by mother and daughter, Maguy and Laetitia. Their wines are made and are aged in the heart of the old village, and include traditional Collioure red and rosé wines, plus a range of Banyuls. They also own vineyards in Côtes du Roussillon.

LOOK FOR:
▸ Banyuls Blanc, with its perfume of lavender and violets
▸ Cuvée Méditerranée Banyuls, a glorious concoction of figs, prunes, roasted almonds, chocolate and coffee
▸ Cuvée Joseph Géraud, an aged, red Banyuls full of the flavour of prunes

DOMAINE DE LA RECTORIE, BANYULS AND COLLIOURE

Around 30 different wines are made at this small property each year from 30 different parcels of land that make up this splendid, 25-ha (62-acre) estate. It is run with great imagination by brothers Marc, Thierry and Pierre Parcé and many consider them to be the leading producers of the area. Their wide range of Banyuls in particular is testament to the hard work they put in to maintaining their vineyards, which are worked by horse and plough rather than machines – the terraces are simply too narrow to support the use of modern machinery.

LOOK FOR:
▸ Le Séris and la Coume Pascole, two age-worthy Collioure reds that are relatively pale in colour. The difference between them is that le Séris is made mainly from the Grenache grape variety whereas la Coume Pascole is a blend of Grenache, Syrah and Carignan
▸ Col del Blast, made from 80 per cent Carignan L'Oriental Banyuls, with a curious yet inviting aroma of coffee and aniseed
▸ Cuvée Parcé Frères, which is a Vintage Banyuls in everything but name because it isn't aged for as long as the local wine laws demand
▸ Cuvée Léon Parcé, aged in oak barrels for 18 months to give a richer style and named in honour of their grandfather
▸ Banyuls Cuvée Pédro Soler, a bone-dry style

Rivesaltes

A 40-km (25-mile) drive north brings you to the town of Rivesaltes. The heavenly, sweet Vins Doux Naturels for which it is famous offers great bargains, most especially the ones made by local co-operatives, because they are somewhat out of fashion at the moment. Grab a chance to taste these delicious, thick, sticky wines if you can because they are some of France's best wines of this style.

Rivesaltes Ambré is produced from the Grenache Blanc and Macabeo grape varieties, while Grenache Noir is the main grape variety behind the strawberry-flavoured, red Rivesaltes Tuilé. Like Banyuls, wines labelled Vintage are bottled when they are young, though the norm is to age them in oak barrels for a couple of years. Rivesaltes Hors d'Age means that the wine has been aged in oak for at least five years. And, yes, you do need the memory of an elephant to remember all the differences in label lore between Rivesaltes and Banyuls. It seems typically French that the two winemaking areas didn't put their heads together to agree on a common form of nomenclature. One of the tastiest and best wines from Rivesaltes, though, is the golden-coloured, aromatic Muscat de Rivesaltes (made largely from the Muscat of Alexandria grape variety) that you drink as young as possible and tastes of runny honey, plump raisins and chunky orange marmalade.

Côtes du Roussillon and Côtes du Roussillon-Villages

Turning inland from Rivesaltes, you'll find yourself in the large sub-region of Côtes du Roussillon, which starts south of Corbières and runs across the Agly valley (which is enjoying the most wonderful renaissance right now) through to the foothills of the Pyrénées. Vines are just about the only form of agriculture that these untamed hills will support. The climate here is very hot and very dry, and it's almost permanently blustery thanks to the northerly Tramontane wind (just one of 13 different winds that plague Languedoc-Roussillon). In the old days, grapes didn't fare too well under these conditions and the wines they created tasted horribly stewed.

Until the mid-1980s, much of the wine production remained in the hands of the village co-operatives. Even the first independent producers struggled to make good wine at first, but a new generation of winemakers is proving the potential of the area and modern Côtes du Roussillon and Côtes du Roussillon-Villages are altogether much improved wines (though it's still best to avoid co-operative wines). The reds are tastier than the whites, on the whole, embracing the smells of charcoal, violets and bay leaves and a rich taste of blackberries and plums.

Côtes du Roussillon-Villages is the better of the two wines because the grapes are sourced from cooler sites up on the hills of the Agly valley in the northwest of the district – indeed, the top four villages (Caramany, Latour-de-France, Lesquerde and Tautavel) are now allowed to add their name to the label. There's a pioneering spirit as the potential of this corner of Roussillon is being developed, particularly as vineyards of ancient Grenache are being rediscovered.

The eastern Pyrénées provide a beautiful backdrop of scenery that makes travelling through this area a pure pleasure, especially in the foothills where you can pick out routes that combine everything – wine, historic towns and mountains. And do stop to taste the Catalan food. For example, boles de picolat (meatballs of minced beef and pork, simmered in a sauce of onions, cinnamon, chilli peppers, olives, tomatoes and ham), escargots Catalans (snails in tomato sauce) and saucisse à la Catalane (sausage fried with garlic, orange peel and herbs) are typical dishes that feature widely on local menus. Talking of which, note that beef stew is called ollada or ouillade in Roussillon. Also try the snails, which the locals pick out of their shells with a nail (the kind you hammer, not the varnished sort).

DOMAINE MATASSA

This new estate is a shining example of the younger, more cosmopolitan generation of winemakers that is moving into Languedoc-Roussillon, buying for a song the vineyards that the retiring local generation cannot farm any more.

South African winemaker Tom Lubbe, who has worked in Bordeaux, South Africa and at the nearby Domaine Gauby, and New Zealander Sam Harrop, who used to be a wine buyer for Marks & Spencer, established Domaine Matassa near the town of Calce in 2001. They were attracted by a small vineyard high up in the hills of the Coteaux des Fenouillèdes, at 450 metres (1476 ft) above sea level, where the air is relatively cool. This, coupled with the favourable granite soils and the old Carignan vines, was enough to convince them to buy it. They have since gone on to purchase a further 12 vineyard plots across 18 different sites and the red wine they now make is a blend of Grenache, Mourvèdre and, of course, the original Carignan. They also make a white wine based mainly on Grenache Blanc.

They bring their combined New World expertise to bear while still respecting the old traditions. They grow their grapes using biodynamic methods (see page 156) and make their wine as simply as possible. Quantities are tiny: just 7200 bottles are produced each year. The wines are dazzling: the white is waxy yet crisp, zesty yet slightly honeyed; the red is all cherries, strawberries and black pepper, with a slightly gamey edge.

These wines would once have been labelled Vin de Pays des Coteaux des Fenouillèdes, but officialdom decided to do away with all but two of the zonal Vins de Pays in the Pyrénées-Orientales department so it is now labelled as plain Vin de Table. Given Matassa's ability to command prices of over £25 a bottle for wines that have only been around for a few years, it seems that its designation matters not a jot. This supports Harrop's belief that the greatest wine of Roussillon will come from the Coteaux des Fenouillèdes in the future.

Minervois

It's time to head north again, to the northeast of Carcassonne, where the Minervois appellation is yet another source of some of the best Languedoc-Roussillon wines. The traditional Vin Doux Naturel Muscat St-Jean de Minervois and the pine-scented, herby and cherry-flavoured reds come from a horseshoe-shaped collection of vineyards squeezed into the rocky, hilly terrain that lies between the Canal du Midi in the south and the Montagne Noire in the north. Co-operatives dominate production and the juicy, easy-drinking wines they make offer great value. Top wines, however, come from a number of individual estates such as Clos Centeilles and Château Tours Boissée. A few are even trying their hand at producing dry white wines from grapes grown high in the foothills of the Montagne Noir where it is considerably cooler. These are worth seeking out for their wonderful scent of lilies and coriander, and rich flavours of quince and dates.

Coteaux du Languedoc

Like Corbières, the vast, rocky, beautiful landscape of the garrigue located between Montpellier and Narbonne also has 15,000 ha (37,000 acres) under vine, producing 73 million bottles of mainly red and rosé wines each year, most of which is pretty good.

The top wines of the region – Faugères, St-Chinian and Clairette de Languedoc – each have their own individual appellations contrôlées and prove the point that the best styles come from grapes grown inland in the foothills of the Cévennes mountains where it is much cooler. Indeed, given the sheer size of this sub-region, there are huge variations in climate from one part to another, and, to this end, the region is currently undergoing a process of re-classification in an attempt to establish some kind of wine hierarchy via a system of climatic zones – in other words, to sort out the good wines from the less good. To this end, seven zones have

LANGUEDOC-ROUSSILLON

83

been identified, but only three of them – Grès de Montpellier, La Clape and Pic St-Loup – are actually allowed to put their name on the label at the moment. La Clape in particular is the wine to look for if you want the scent of violets and herbs and the flavours of plums, black cherries and liquorice. Pic St-Loup also makes some of Languedoc-Roussillon's top red wines.

All these wines are extremely food-friendly, which is just as well because the cuisine of this part of Languedoc-Roussillon is very varied and is influenced by the warmth of the Mediterranean and the harsher climate of the mountains. Near the coast, dishes prepared à la Languedocienne are cooked with aubergines, tomatoes and garlic. Inland, however, pork, wild mushrooms, truffles, dried beans, lentils and chestnuts are common ingredients (try cousinat, a rich chestnut and cream soup). The local lamb and mutton are good, often tasting of the herbs that grow in the pastures where the animals graze – look for lamb sous la mère, which is suckling lamb raised in the mountains of Lozère and the Pyrénées. Alternatively, sample the delights of petits pâtés de Pézénas, a small, sweet and savoury pie containing roast mutton, brown sugar and lemon zest.

As in other French regions, there is also a wide variety of delicious cheeses. Try Pélardon des Cévennes, one of the oldest goat's-milk cheeses of Europe, manufactured for many centuries. This has a lovely creamy texture, sometimes with blue or white mould on its crust, and is heavy with the scent of the gorse, heather and grass on which the goats feed. Interestingly, for many years goat's cheese suffered an image problem because the goat was considered the poor man's cow. How times have changed. Today, Pélardon is highly sought after and has its own appellation contrôlée.

Other wine names to seek out include Picpoul de Pinet, a crisp, citrussy and slightly nutty white wine that is delicious with the local fish and seafood. Muscat de Frontignan, Muscat de Mireval and Muscat de Lunel are all good Vins Doux Naturels.

That's more like it – a big plate of simple pork and chips.

MAS DE DAUMAS GASSAC,
VIN DE PAYS DE L'HÉRAULT

This is perhaps the ultimate example of a Vin de Pays – indeed, when the wine was first released in 1978, it was declared the Lafite of the Languedoc. This acclamation is made even more startling when you think that the domaine had no history of growing grapes and making wine – indeed, no-one had ever planted vines in the Gassac valley before.

The estate is owned by Aimé Guibert, who used to be a glove manufacturer and leather processor. He and his wife bought the property in 1971 in order to cut down on the time it took him to commute to and from work. One of the couple's best friends, Professor Henri Enjalbert, happened to be an expert on the geology of vineyards and, on first visiting the property, spotted its potential immediately, describing the soil as a geological miracle. Not able to resist the challenge, the couple hired top winemaking-consultant Professor Emile Peynaud of Bordeaux University to advise them on what to plant and how to make wine. He proposed Cabernet Sauvignon and this, coupled with the fact that Peynaud made the first two vintages, gave a wine that was very Bordeaux-like in style.

Cabernet Sauvignon continues to be the mainstay of the red Mas de Daumas Gassac (that positively demands aging for ten to 15 years) and Viognier, Muscat, Chardonnay and Petit Manseng are used for the white. Guibert can experiment with as many different grape varieties as he pleases, in fact, because the property lies outside of any of the Languedoc-Roussillon appellations (hence it can only be labelled as a Vin de Pays). Alongside the varieties mentioned above, he grows Syrah, Pinot Noir, Merlot, Malbec, Cabernet Franc, Tannat, Grenache, Tempranillo, Nebbiolo, Barbera and Dolcetto plus a range of rather obscure varieties, including Neher Leschol from the Middle East and Voskehat from Armenia, across 50 vineyard plots scattered through 80 ha (200 acres) of land.

LOOK FOR:
▸ Cuvée Emile Peynaud, the very top wine made from the oldest Cabernet Sauvignon vines
▸ Vin de Laurance, a glorious sweet white wine

LES DOMAINES PAUL MAS,
COTEAUX DU LANGUEDOC

Les Domaines Paul Mas is a group of four estates (Château Paul Mas, Domaine de Nicole, Mas de la Bergerie and Domaine de l'île de Conas) covering 81 ha (200 acres) of vineyards on the hills bordering the Hérault valley, close to the small town of Pézenas in the heart of Coteaux du Languedoc. The Mas family has owned these for more than 100 years. Today, Jean-Claude Mas stands at the helm of this innovative and dynamic company that produces six million bottles of wine every year.

A daring man, he is not afraid to experiment with different grapes in the search for excellence, making stylish, vibrant wines that have one foot planted firmly in the local soils and the other turned towards the New World (very soft and fruity wines, in other words). Indeed, his motto is 'Old World wines with New World attitude'.

They also own the Domaine Astruc winery in Malras near Limoux, where they create their 'dA' range of wines as well as Vin de Pays d'Oc varietal wines. It's much cooler here, so the wines are more restrained and elegant in personality.

A large number of wines are made that are sold under a range of different label names, such as Paul Mas Vignes de Nicole, dA, Château Paul Mas, Claude Val, La Forge Estate, Hidden Hill and Mas de la Bergerie. Some are created from a blend of grapes while others are varietals. The Syrah, Grenache, Cabernet Sauvignon, Merlot, Carignan and Cinsaut grape varieties are used to make the red wines. The whites are created from Viognier, Marsanne, Sauvignon Blanc and Chardonnay. Each range reflects the terroir of the vineyards in which the grapes used to make them are grown.

They also make very fruity Vin de Pays d'Oc wines called Arrogant Frog (Ribet red, Ribet rosé and Ribet white) in recognition of the terrible snobbery that is often associated with French wine and its producers (with which he has no truck). And another tongue-in-cheek label – Que Sera Sirah, a barrel-aged Vin de Pays d'Oc made from (you've guessed it) the Syrah grape variety.

Costières de Nîmes

WHEN TO DRINK THE WINES OF SOUTHERN FRANCE
▸ Corbières and Fitou improve for five years or more from the vintage date
▸ Red Collioures are good when young, but can be aged for a decade.
▸ Banyuls can be kept for a decade or more
▸ Vins Doux Naturels can live for 20 to 30 years

The trip through the Languedoc-Roussillon region ends in a rather odd area that lies between Nîmes and the Rhône delta. By convention, it's always counted as part of Languedoc-Roussillon but, politically and administratively, Costières de Nîmes is part of the Rhône region. Furthermore, the character of the tasty red wines this district produces is very similar in style and taste to those of the southern Rhône wine region – fruity, fleshy and warm-hearted. As if this weren't enough, topographically there are many similarities with the southern Rhône in that the land is low and is covered with the same kind of heat-retaining stones found in Châteauneuf-du-Pape (see page 117) – indeed, the climate of Costières de Nîmes is one of the hottest in France.

The district's white and rosé wines have improved greatly over recent years, the direct result of heavy investment in the wineries. Without modern winemaking equipment to control fermentation temperatures, it is virtually impossible to create refreshing, aromatic white and rosé wines in very hot climates. Runaway fermentation temperatures strip away perfume and flavour, giving very flabby and dull wines.

Better white wines are great news from the eating point of view in that there are now some local white wines worth drinking with your fruits de mer (literally, fruits of the sea). The salt-water lagoons that line the Languedoc coast are not only a breeding ground for flamingos but also for shellfish and seafood – order a plateful of oysters, mussels, sea urchins, cockles, sea snails and tellines (tiny clams). Another great speciality of Nîmes is brandade de morue, which is puréed salted cod combined with olive oil and garlic.

You might also see some Camargue specialities on the menu when you're in this district. For example, Camargue beef comes from two breeds of fighting bull that are bred in the Camargue and in the mountain regions of the Pyrénées, Aubrac, Cévennes and Margeride. Their meat is used for a dish called gardiane, which is a casserole of the beef with vegetables, black olives, garlic, smoked bacon and red wine.

Food and wine matching

As you might expect, the wines of Languedoc-Roussillon go well with Mediterranean and North African dishes, such as chicken cooked in tomatoes and garlic, stuffed peppers or tomatoes, couscous, beef or lamb tagines, garlic mushrooms, Spanish tortilla and lamb marinated in olive oil, lemon juice and garlic.

Having mentioned garlic here a few times, a simple Vin de Pays d'Oc Chardonnay works well with garlic sausage and garlicky pâtés. And Vin de Pays d'Oc Chardonnay also works its magic with smoked haddock, leek-based quiches, creamy onion soup, roast pork, salmon terrine, lemon sole and trout with almonds.

REGIONAL-FOOD SPECIALITIES
▸ Aligot – a purée made from potatoes and cheese, seasoned with garlic
▸ Olives – the best are called Picholine and Lucque
▸ Encornets farcis – squid stuffed with meat, bread, egg, garlic and parsley, cooked in a tomato sauce and served with Camargue rice
▸ Bourride de Sète – monkfish, cuttlefish or squid simmered in white wine, which is thickened with garlic mayonnaise before being served on a bed of toasted bread
▸ Gigot de mer à la palavasienne – monkfish served with ratatouille

What is wine? by James

Wine is a very simple concoction. Grapes grow on vines and achieve ripeness in the late summer or early autumn. They are picked (usually by students) and thrown into a big vat. Here they are pressed so that the juice runs out into another vat.

The basic process is exactly the same wherever wine is made. You may find bucolic former resistance leaders in a remote French farmhouse, treading whatever grapes the Good Lord has sent them in an old barrel and singing 'Gentil'. This wine is often served in a bucket.

You may also find an aristocrat in a superb château, ruling over a single domaine and managing the harvests of specific grapes very carefully to produce an appellation wine of enormous expense. Very small quantities of this wine are served in terrifyingly fragile long-stemmed glasses to visiting television presenters, and often rather reluctantly at that. But they have both done the same thing – squashed grapes and left nature to perform its miraculous alchemy, just as the Romans, the Persians and the Ancient Greeks did.

However, there is a difference. The wine from the farmer's bucket, the wine of the merry peasant, produced only for the pleasure of his own family and unadulterated by the pressures of commerce, fashion or even bottling, tastes unremittingly foul.

Another rustic wine that might be worth considering instead is Domaine de Voiture 2006, just one litre of which was made in the boot of our Jaguar, and is thus an English wine. No wine grapes were available so table grapes were used, to which were added baker's yeast and sugar lumps stolen from a hotel. Fermentation took place in a used mineral water bottle over five days. But it, too, was revolting.

Yet the château wine, ostensibly made in the same way, is superb. How so? Because although the toff in charge might like to present an image of time-honoured pre-industrial innocence, the reality is somewhat different and may be seen hidden away in the cave. Here you will find boffins in white coats who seem to have been smuggled out of Werner Von Braun's V2 rocket project, wielding clipboards and laptops, ministering to huge control panels of blinking lights and moving ghost-like through a sterile world of stainless steel. Where it matters, science and technology are allowed to triumph over the rural idyll.

So wine is not the joyous God-given elixir we imagine it to be. In its basic form it is a dreadful drink – harsh, bitter, full of tannin and barely tolerable unless accompanied by strong food. But a few people, through wit, cunning, and even deviousness, have managed to turn it into something palatable.

Beer is much more reliable.

CHAPTER 3 **PROVENCE**

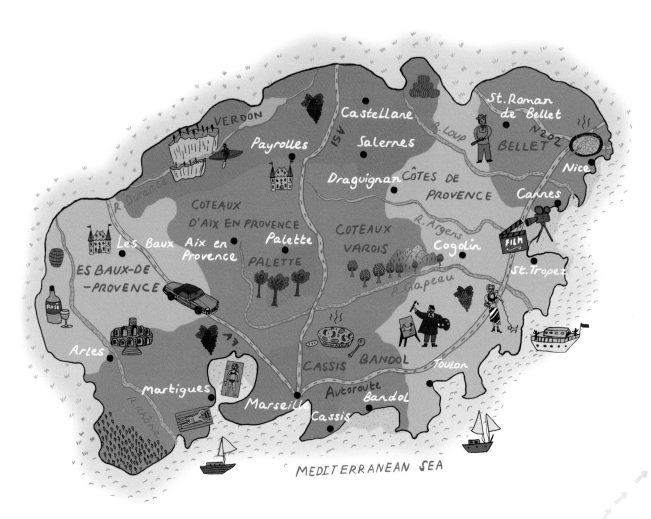

VERDON

St. Roman
de Bellet

Castellane

Payrolles

Salernes

BELLET

N 202

ISV

R. Loup

Nice

Draguignan

Côtes de
Provence

COTEAUX
D'AIX EN PROVENCE

Cannes

Les Baux

Aix en
Provence

Palette

COTEAUX
VAROIS

R. Argens

Cogolin

ES BAUX-DE
-PROVENCE

PALETTE

St. Tropez

R. Durance

R. Gapeau

ROSE

Arles

Martigues

CASSIS   BANDOL

Toulon

R. Rhône

Marseille

Autoroute   Bandol

Cassis

MEDITERRANEAN SEA

FILM

With its famous film festival, private yachts and reputation for high living, there isn't anywhere else in France that is quite so swanky as Provence. It's also an outstandingly beautiful part of the country that for centuries has attracted famous artists, such as Cézanne and Van Gogh, thanks to intensely blue skies that afford a very special kind of light. The Mistral (see page 114) blows away the clouds, leaving the sun to shine for 3000 hours each year.

This land of mountainous countryside covered in lavender and wild, aromatic herbs is also one of France's top holiday destinations for its quaint and colourful fishing ports, sandy beaches, azure sea, guaranteed summertime heat and, of course, the delicious Provençal cuisine du soleil ('cuisine of the sun') made from the freshest of local ingredients.

So where do wines fit into the picture? Well, vines were first planted here in 600 BC by the Phoenicians, making Provence the oldest wine region of France. Winemaking flourished under the Romans who organized the local population into efficient communities and settlements, such as Arles, Aix-en-Provence, Marseille and Nice, to name but a few, the very places to which the tourists flock today. Nevertheless it is perfectly reasonable to question whether the wine industry would have survived here if it hadn't been for those same tourists clamouring for something to drink because Provence is awash in an ocean of deeply uninspiring wines on the whole, most of it rosé in colour. Indeed, it speaks volumes that the first appellations contrôlées of the region weren't created until 1936, which was pretty late by French wine standards, and the sub-regional appellations were set up even later than this (as late as 1977

for Côtes de Provence, for example). Unfortunately, there isn't much of an incentive to change this state of affairs because too many producers know that their wine will sell, whatever its quality – and they often flog them at ridiculously high prices.

Having said this, though, there's a growing band of dedicated winemakers who are coaxing far superior wines from small pockets of land, often in places where vines have never been cultivated before. Most of these are red in colour, made from blends of the Syrah, Grenache, Mourvèdre, Carignan, Cinsaut and Cabernet Sauvignon grape varieties, which are very well suited to the hot, dry climate of Provence. So why aren't more white wines made? Well, in many places, especially near the coast where it's scorching hot, it's often simply too much of a climatic challenge to go to the effort of growing white grapes, even though the Mistral helps to cool things down as it rips through the region. The white-grape varieties cultivated – mainly Clairette, Grenache Blanc, Sémillon, Ugni Blanc and Rolle (which is another name for Vermentino) – ripen too easily here and it's hard to retain their acidity, so the wines they make tend to taste unappetizingly flabby.

With some 26,000 ha (64,220 acres) under vine, the Provence wine region is enormous. It stretches from the town of Arles just to the east of the river Rhône right round to the Italian border. Many of the vineyards hug the coastline, but vines are also cultivated far into the mountain foothills inland. The very best wines are crafted in the small areas of Bandol, Bellet, Cassis, Les Baux-de-Provence and Palette (each with its own appellation contrôlée), but most of Provence's wine hails from the much larger, catch-all appellations of Côtes de Provence and Coteaux d'Aix-en-Provence. The vast majority of it is dull wine, rarely offering any excitement. As ever, though, there are a few shining exceptions: Domaine Richeaume in Côtes de Provence produces one of Provence's finest red wines (a Cabernet Sauvignon, Syrah and Merlot blend called Cuvée Columelle); while in Coteaux d'Aix-en-Provence, Château Vignelaure has made quite a name for itself (see page 100).

The beaches of Provence are so crowded that many of the local beauties are forced to sunbathe upside down on a cliff face.

The making of rosés

Contrary to popular belief, the vast majority of pink wines are not made by mixing red and white wines together. In fact, they start off life being treated as if they were going to be red wines. After the grapes have arrived at the winery, they are de-stemmed and crushed, and the juice, pulp and skins are then pumped into a fermentation vessel (usually constructed of stainless steel).

The must (as this thick soup of juice, pulp and skins is described) starts bubbling away as the yeasts get to work on the grape sugars. The rising temperature of the must – heat is released during the fermentation process – helps to draw out colour and tannin from the skins and the fermenting wine soon takes on a pinkish hue. It's fairly obvious that the liquid is drained of the solids as soon as the desired amount of colour has been acquired.

After this, it is handled as if it were a white wine: it is pumped into another stainless-steel vat, where fermentation continues at a much lower temperature in order to retain whatever subtle nuance of aroma and flavour there is.

The best of Provence

If you're starting your journey through Provence at Arles (famous for its pork sausage that also used to include donkey meat), the first place to visit is the enchanting village of Les Baux. This lies at the centre of the tiny Les Baux-de-Provence appellation nestled into the foothills of the Alpilles mountains (which translates as the 'Alplets'). Bauxite, the primary source of aluminium, was named after Les Baux, where it was first discovered in 1821, and when you look at the rocky land it seems hard to believe that vines can be grown successfully here. But a dozen or so individual producers, such as Domaine de Trévallon (see page 100), work their magic to create some stunning, very fruity, soft yet full-bodied red wines from blends of Syrah, Cabernet Sauvignon and Grenache. They also make some of the best rosé wines in Provence. This is one of the hottest and driest parts of France and so it is pretty easy for the growers to farm their vineyards organically – the lack of rain and the strong heat mean that grapes grown here are rarely affected by problems of rot and, therefore, the grape growers do not need to use the chemical sprays that must be applied in damper areas where rot is an ever-present threat. There are very good olive oils on sale in this area, too, by the way.

TASTING NOTES
Côtes de Provence Rosé, Domaine Houchart, 2005
Oz says: This is good – it's full with a nice acidity. There's gentle apple fruit and some strawberries thrown in.
James says: This could almost have been made by Trebor. It has that slight taste of penny sweets about it. Not bad, though.

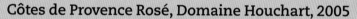

DOMAINE DE TRÉVALLON

This domaine, named after the three valleys at the back of the property, lies in the far north of Les Baux near St-Rémy-de-Provence. It is run by the pioneering Eloi Dürrbach who, in 1973, was the first to plant vines in the Alpilles. It was his father, René, a painter and sculptor, who actually bought the Trévallon farmhouse, back in 1955 when he was looking for somewhere peaceful to live. A godson of Pablo Picasso, no less, he designed the memorable labels for the wines. The farmhouse is set in 60 ha (148 acres) of rocky scrubland and the task of clearing the land and carving vineyards out of the rock was Herculean (in fact, the rock had to be broken up with dynamite).

Today, the fabulous, herby, succulent, blackcurranty and plummy red wine of this estate – and one of the most thrilling wines in France – is made from 60 per cent Cabernet Sauvignon and 40 per cent Syrah. Fine so far. Except that there is too much Cabernet Sauvignon in the blend according to the local wine laws, so it can only be labelled as Vin de Pays des Bouches-du-Rhône. His splendid, honeyed, barrel-fermented white wine created from a blend of Roussanne and Marsanne grape varieties also falls foul of the local wine laws, so this, too, can only be labelled Vin de Pays. Dürrbach has also been refused permission to extend his vineyard.

CHÂTEAU VIGNELAURE, COTEAUX D'AIX-EN-PROVENCE

Son of Irishman Vincent O'Brien (regarded by many as the greatest racehorse trainer Ireland has ever produced), David O'Brien was also a top-class trainer through the 1980s – indeed, in 1984 he became the youngest trainer to win the Epsom Derby with Secreto, beating his father's horse, El Gran Senor, by a short head.

He always knew that he wanted to own a winery and started off by working in the vineyards of the showcase Château Vignelaure – 'the vineyard of the sacred spring' – set high in the beautiful, wild hills to the north of Aix-en-Provence, close to where *Jean de Florette* was filmed. The other workers were completely flabbergasted when he went on to buy the estate in 1994 because they had absolutely no idea of his background.

The château's first claim to fame was in 1965 when it was bought by the innovative Georges Brunet, who was responsible for turning around the fortunes of Château Lagune in Bordeaux. He was the first person to plant Cabernet Sauvignon in Provence and the estate quickly established a fine reputation throughout the world. Even today, many of the wines are dominated by this grape variety, wines that can age easily for 15 to 20 years.

The wines are created by freelance winemaker Richard Osbourne, a larger than life, plain-talking Australian who has been making wine in France for 18 years. Having been boss of his own winery at the tender age of 20, he decided to set off around the world and made wine in places such as Spain and Chile before deciding to settle in Provence. His impact on many of the wineries at which he consults has been enormous.

Château Vignelaure is open to the public for tastings and tours of the cellars and vineyards all year round, and it has a wine shop where you can buy its wines.

LOOK FOR:

▶ Château Vignelaure, the top red wine of the estate, made from grapes from old vines, and the jewel in the crown of the Coteaux d'Aix-en-Provence appellation

▶ L'Esprit de Vignelaure, a Vin de Pays crafted mainly from Cabernet Sauvignon

▶ La Colline de Vignelaure, a Vin de Pays made mainly from Merlot and named after the dry, rocky hillside where the vines grow

▶ Château Vignelaure rosé, a rich and complex wine, first produced in 2003

▶ La Source de Vignelaure, an easy-drinking style of red

▶ Esprit de Nijinsky red, which pays homage to the very first harvest of the Cabernet Sauvignon vines in 1970 along with the legendary racehorse

▶ Nijinsky, trained by Vincent O'Brien, which won the Triple Crown in the same year

If one of your stops is in Aix-en-Provence, look for some of the regional gastronomic specialities, such as pan bagna (meaning 'bathed bread'), which is a baguette filled with tuna, tomato, peppers and black olives, all steeped in an olive oil, white-wine vinegar, Dijon mustard and garlic dressing. Wash this down with a glass of white Château Simone, which hails from the appellation of Palette, located in the thick of the nearby Aleppo pine forests. Don't be tempted by the red and rosé wines, however; they tend to taste of the resin from the pine needles that litter the floors of the vineyards.

If you're raring to go to the coast, drive down to the pretty fishing port of Cassis, just a few miles to the east of Marseille. This is the perfect place to sit in one of the fashionable quayside restaurants to enjoy the freshest-possible fish and shellfish – everything from sardines, red mullet, tuna, monkfish, sea bass, red snapper and anchovies to shrimps, crab, oysters and palourdes (a kind of clam). These are often accompanied by raïto (often spelled 'rayte'), a sauce made from red wine, tomatoes, garlic and ground walnuts.

One fish dish that is hugely popular with the locals is bouillabaisse, a robust, stew that originated in Marseille and is often served as a cele-bratory meal. It can be made from a varying mix of fish including all the fish mentioned above as well as salt cod, lobster, conger eel, scorpion fish and gurnard, plus the obligatory saffron, fennel seeds, garlic and bitter orange peel. The soup and the fish are usually served in separate bowls, the soup being poured over slices of toasted French bread, all topped with a dollop of chilli and garlic mayonnaise called rouille.

The refreshing, local white wine is ideal with this kind of food and you won't even need to leave your seat to gaze up at the vines that created them. Be prepared to pay through your nose for it, however; these wines are much in demand locally and there are only 175 ha (432 acres) under vine here, so supply doesn't always meet demand (which always equals high prices). So are they worth it? Well, no, not really. In fact, a simple phrase sums up the wines of Cassis: what a rip-off. But, hey, you're on holiday, aren't you?

You could now travel eastwards along the coast to yet another picturesque fishing port, Bandol, where the spectacular, terraced

vineyards that form an amphitheatre around the port are renowned for producing some of Provence's top red and rosé wines. Here, the Mourvèdre grape variety is king, thanks to ideal growing conditions (where it can soak up the sun and the heat to ripen to perfection), and it makes up 50 per cent of the blend of the ageworthy, herby, truffley and raisiny red wines. The rosés taste of spiced, ripe strawberries, though once again they are rather pricey for what they are.

Red Bandol is the kind of wine that goes well with the regional recipes that use lamb as an ingredient. For example, pieds et paquets à la Provençale is lambs' feet simmered in a tomato and wine sauce served with 'packages' of lamb stomach stuffed with green bacon, chopped garlic and a pinch of hillside herbs. Perhaps more akin to the British taste of things, you could drink Bandol with épaule d'agneau farcie au thon, which is shoulder of lamb stuffed with green and black olives, bacon, tuna, hard-boiled eggs and herbs.

If you've had enough coast and wine, take the high road that winds through the Maures mountains towards Draguignan. Thoughts of wine cannot be abandoned entirely, however, because you will be able to see the cork-oak trees, as well as the chestnut trees that provide the source for the local marrons glacés (sugar-coated chestnuts). From Draguignan, it is not very far to the famous Gorges du Verdon, Europe's answer to the Grand Canyon.

No trip to Provence would be complete without dipping your toes into the Mediterranean from the glorious Côte d'Azur beaches of St-Tropez, Cannes or Nice. Here you can sip the fresh, aromatic white wines of Bellet, another tiny area with only 44 ha (108 acres) of vines, which lies in the Alpine foothills to the north of Nice. Needless to say by now, it is laughably overpriced. As far as local food specialities are concerned, Italian influences are beginning to be felt now (Nice is very close to the Italian border, after all) and there is wide use of pasta, especially ravioli, cannelloni and gnocchi. Try pissaladière, which is a type of pizza topped with onions, olives, anchovies and Provençal herbs. There's also soupe au pistou, a type of bean and vegetable soup to which a crushed paste of fresh basil, garlic, Parmesan cheese and olive oil is stirred in at the last moment (pistou is the French for 'pesto', both of which mean 'pestle').

COTEAUX VAROIS
Centred around the town of Brignoles, which is located well inland to the north of Toulon, the Coteaux Varois makes wines that demonstrate what can be achieved when Cabernet Sauvignon, Syrah, Grenache, Cinsaut and Mourvèdre vines are planted at a higher and cooler altitude in the Provence region. Put simply, they are much better. As growers work to plant exactly the right grape variety in exactly the right site, these wines can only improve even further in quality. This is definitely one to watch.

VIN DE PAYS DES BOUCHES-DU-RHÔNE

As both Domaine de Trévallon and Château Vignelaure prove (see page 100), some very good wines are forced to be declassified from appellation-contrôlée to Vin de Pays status simply because they are made in breach of local wine laws. This could be because there is too high a percentage of one particular grape variety in the blend, or, perhaps, a grape variety has been used that is not permitted for the appellation at all.

Either way, the winemaker is afforded more freedom by electing to adopt the lower status (because the rules aren't so demanding) and it gives him or her the chance to experiment with new grape varieties. For example, the obscure Marselan and Chasan varieties have been used to create wines labelled Vin de Pays des Bouches-du-Rhône. These hit the UK shelves in 2003, yet they have already won awards for their high quality. Keep an eye on these wines.

WHEN TO DRINK THE WINES OF PROVENCE

As a rule, the majority of Provencal wines are designed to be drunk as soon as they are ready. The exceptions are the top-quality red wines from Les Baux-de-Provence and Bandol. These can be opened three to four years after the date of vintage, but very often last for many years more.

Food and wine matching

White and rosé Provence wines make good, all-round summer drinking. But if you want to be more adventurous about matching Provence wines with specific foods, try the rosés with Chinese-style chicken wings, borscht (Russian beetroot soup), rabbit in cider, stuffed aubergine and any type of fish soup (but most especially lobster bisque).

If you're in the mood for red wine, red Coteaux-d'Aix-en-Provence and Côtes de Provence wines are good with pilchards in tomato sauce served on hot buttered toast, stuffed peppers, moussaka, liver and bacon, nut roast and sausage and mash. Bandol is particularly tasty with steak and kidney pie or beef braised in red wine. It's also a great partner to many game dishes, such as rabbit and guinea fowl, and the more robust pigeon, wild duck, roast grouse, pheasant casserole, roast woodcock, jugged hare and venison casserole.

Menu items listed as 'à la Provençale' invariably means that tomatoes, garlic, olive oil, onions and herbs are used to make it. Anything described as 'à la Niçoise' also includes olives and anchovies, at the very least. For example, a typical salade Niçoise usually contains tuna, potatoes, green beans, lettuce, tomatoes, onion, anchovies, hard-boiled eggs and black olives, all seasoned with a traditional French dressing.

Vegetables are often baked or fried in olive oil for dishes such as ratatouille. From the French word 'touiller', which means to stir around or mix, ratatouille is commonly made up of tomatoes, onions, courgettes, aubergine, peppers, squash and basil, and is served either hot as a side dish with meat, or cold as a starter or salad.

Tapenade, a Provençal speciality, is a paste made with olive oil, olives, anchovies, capers and garlic, which is typically spread on bread, or served with grilled fish or chicken.

Terroir by Oz

I should have seen this coming. The moment when I tried to introduce James to the concept of {terroir}. 'Tairwahh', he hooted, doing his level best to mangle a perfectly simple word and, with completely unnecessary facial contortions, coming out with a mess of syllables and diphthongs that sounded as though he had a mouth full of blotting paper. The great founts of righteous indignation at anything that seems to him even remotely pretentious boil endlessly directly beneath his calm exterior. And there is nothing like a French 'concept' to set him off.

'So what does ëterroirí mean in English?' he asked. Well, the trouble is there is no direct translation for {terroir} in English. We don't have an equivalent word. It's sort of… oh, why am I bothering?

'Ok. It's a sense of place. This "Je ne sais quoi" in a wine that adds an extra dimension of flavour over and above the flavour of the grape variety. The earth itself. The vineyard. Sometimes you think you can actually taste the vineyard.' But he's not listening. He's off on another of his Francophobic rants about communism and the French Resistance and this gigantic Gallic plot to confuse and cheat the fine, upstanding 'fiver a bottle and not a penny more' hordes of British wine drinkers. And I shouldn't have said 'Je ne sais quoi'. Far too hoity toity. Isn't there an honest Anglo Saxon phrase I could have used instead?

'Oh James, do shut up. Listen.' Trying to get James to embrace any concept outside his tight little world of carburettors, pork pies and a quiet pint at his local is like trying to force a hyperactive five year old to eat his spinach.

'Let's think of it as a sense of place. Every gardener knows that some plots of land produce the most fragment roses. It's just the same with wines. Each grape variety ripens at a different pace, and needs more or less sun and heat and moisture to give the tastiest crop.

But it's not just soil. It's the aspect of the land to the sun. It's the protection provided by the forest or mountain range from rain and squalls and storm. It's the direction the vines are planted in, how they're pruned, what crop they bear, whether the grapes are picked underripe, overripe or just so. And how the wine is made. What vision of flavour a winemaker has; an ego-driven determination to stamp his own identity on the wine, or a sensitive longing to let the wine express the place, the {terroir}. And when it's there you can taste it.'

'Oh yes', says James. What a grand idea. Let's go off and find some stones to lick.

He's like a child, he really is.

CHAPTER 4 **THE RHÔNE VALLEY**

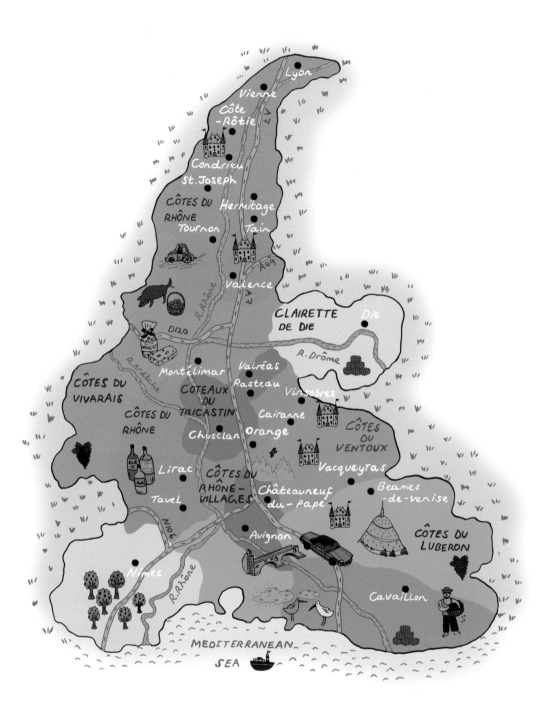

Lyon

Vienne

Côte
-Rôtie

Condrieu

St.Joseph

CÔTES DU
RHÔNE
Tournon

Hermitage

Tain

A49

Valence

CLAIRETTE
DE DIE

Die

D120

R.Rhône

R.Drôme

Montélimar

Valréas

Rasteau

Vinsobres

CÔTES DU
VIVARAIS

R.Ardèche

COTEAUX
DU
TRICASTIN

Cairanne

CÔTES
DU
VENTOUX

CÔTES DU
RHÔNE

Chusclan

Orange

Lirac

CÔTES DU
RHÔNE -
VILLAGES

Châteauneuf
du - pape

Vacqueyras

Beames
-de-venise

Tavel

Gard

Avignon

CÔTES DU
LUBERON

Nîmes

R.Rhône

Cavaillon

MEDITERRANEAN
SEA

For over 2000 years, the vineyards that straddle some 160 km (124 miles) of the Rhône valley in the southeast of France have been an exciting source of wines of almost every style imaginable – oceans of full-bodied, spicy reds, a handful of thrilling, fragrant whites, some excellent rosés, a few good sparklers and, not to forget, a couple of sweet dessert wines.

The powerful river Rhône begins its life in Switzerland before coursing west into France, turning and twisting its way south at Lyon before spilling into the Mediterranean through the wild Camargue swamps near Marseille. The official appellation-contrôlée wine region (the second largest in France after Bordeaux) stretches between Vienne and Avignon only, though there is plenty of Vin de Pays territory running from Avignon down to the sea (albeit that most of this conventionally forms part of the Provence region).

Soils and climate vary along the way, where a craggy, rugged, precipitous landscape studded with peach and nut trees in the north gives way to a wider, flatter, sun-scorched herbal scrubland peppered with olive groves, fruit orchards and lavender fields. The north of the region enjoys a classic continental climate of hot summers and cold winters, but south of Montélimar (famous for its nougat – there's even a nougat museum in this attractive little town), the climate has turned Mediterranean, with hot, dry summers and mild, wet winters. It's not surprising, then, that different vines are planted to suit the natural environment and that the character of the wines changes as the river drifts downstream.

ROUTES TOURISTIQUES DES CÔTES DU RHÔNE
By way of a shining example to the rest of France's wine regions, there are now nine separate, colour-coded wine routes throughout the Rhône valley and its environs. The Saffron Route, for example, covers the vineyards of northern Rhône, with suggestions for 30 different destinations where wineries welcome visitors for tastings. The user-friendly, English-language (albeit shaky in places), wine-tourism pages at www.vins-rhone.com show the details of each route and provide all the information you'll need about cellar opening times and so on.

Key white-grape varieties

Marsanne creates full-bodied, honeyed wines with wonderful aromas of hawthorn flower. It is a much under-rated variety, even though it is one of the grape varieties used to make St-Joseph and Hermitage whites.

Muscat Blanc à Petits Grains is turned into rich, sweet wines in the Rhône (the most famous being Muscat de Beaumes de Venise), which are all syrup, honey, rose petals and orange marmalade.

Roussanne is a difficult grape variety to grow, but is worth the trouble for its aromas of hawthorn flowers and flavours of honey and apricot. Like Marsanne, it is used in the blend to create St-Joseph and Hermitage whites.

Viognier is famous for producing the sensational, aromatic and fruity northern Rhône whites of Condrieu and Château-Grillet that revel in the haunting fragrance of a bouquet of spring flowers, may blossom and honeysuckle, and heavenly flavours of fresh apricots, pears, peaches, sour cream, all underpinned by a mouth-tingling, grapefruity acidity.

TASTING NOTES
Château Courac, Côtes de Rhone, 2002
Oz says: This is quite full, rich and round. There's a bit of leather and grape skin, plus a slight hint of tobacco. Not bad. Gutsy, but not very refreshing.
James says: Yuck. No. There's hair care product or deodorant or something. Yes, it's just like an aerosol deodorant that you've aimed in the wrong direction and it's gone in your mouth.

Key red-grape varieties

Carignan loves the heat of the southern Rhône and needs it, in fact, if it is to ripen properly. It is only ever used as part of a blend, to which it adds acidity and colour.

Cinsault is another grape variety that is only used in blends here in the Rhône valley, where it lends suppleness by smoothing out the high alcohol of Grenache and the astringency of Carignan.

Grenache thrives in the hot conditions of the southern Rhône valley, giving perfumed, herby reds and rosés that boast high alcohol and rich, pepper-strewn flavours of raspberry, blackberry and toffee. It is the major ingredient of the warm and juicy, southern Rhône reds, such as Châteauneuf-du-Pape, Gigondas, Vacqueyras and Côtes du Rhône.

Mourvèdre adds a herby aroma and taste as well as wild-blackberry flavours. It's very much a grape variety of the south of the region because it won't ripen north of Châteauneuf-du-Pape.

Syrah cannot be beaten for its unique fusion of different aromas and flavours – whispers of smoke, spices and wild rosemary and thyme, and the taste of blackberries, raspberries, damsons, loganberries, black treacle, liquorice, black pepper, cherry jam and creamy chocolate. And this is just for starters. This wine is always rich and full-bodied and can be extremely inky and tannic when first bottled, so it certainly wants to be stashed away for a few years before it is ready to drink. Top examples of Syrah-based Rhône wines are Côte-Rôtie, Hermitage and St-Joseph, though it is also the grape variety behind Cornas, Crozes-Hermitage and Coteaux du Tricastin.

Journeying through the south

The southern half of the Rhône region is responsible for 94 per cent of the region's wines. Here, where the valley is wide and the terrain more forgiving, attractive whites and warm-hearted, fleshy reds are produced, almost always from a blend of different grape varieties. The celebrated red Châteauneuf-du-Pape, for instance, can be made from up to 13 different varieties (eight red and five white). The most important is Grenache, followed closely by Cinsault, Mourvèdre, Carignan and Syrah (which is now playing a more defining role in southern Rhône red blends). All these grapes revel in the summertime heat, ripening easily if the vines are planted on the flat river plains, but giving more exciting flavours from the slopes, particularly to the east of the river.

The easy-drinking, juicy and spicy Côtes du Rhône is produced throughout the entire region, but the vast majority of the two million hl (44 million gal.) produced each year comes from the south – and most of it is red. These wines can contrast wildly in character, however – from light and fruity to rich and full-bodied – and the only real way to judge what you are buying is to consider its price: the more you spend, the more you should get. In theory, versions labelled Côtes du Rhône-Villages ought to be better because 70 villages deemed to have superior soils supply the grape varieties used to create them. In reality, though, many merely contain a slightly higher level of alcohol. To guarantee a step up in quality, look for one of the 15 Côtes du Rhône-Villages wines that have a specific village name printed on their label – Sablet-Côtes du Rhône-Villages, for example. The best of these is Cairanne (for both red and white wines), followed closely by Beaumes-de-Venise, Rasteau, Séguret, Valréas and Visan.

THE MISTRAL
The Mistral is an almost permanent, fierce and cold northwesterly wind that is funnelled down the Rhône valley from the Alps. In the north of the region, each vine needs to be staked because the wind is at gale force here, though the hills afford some protection to south-facing vineyards. The flatter south of the region, though, doesn't have this luxury and therefore experiences the full blast of the wind. You will notice banks of tall reeds that are grown specifically as anti-Mistral windbreaks and most of the vines are usually trained close to the ground. The one advantage this wind does offer is that it dries the grapes really quickly after a downpour, so rot is rarely a problem here.

French cyclists are one of the many hazards facing the unsuspecting foreign motorist.

DOMAINE VIRET, ST-MAURICE-SUR-EYGUES

The idea of applying organic principles to grape-growing doesn't attract the sniggers that it once did, possibly because so many modern growers have adopted them. Given, however, that the jury is still out when it comes to biodynamic viticulture (see page 156), it's no wonder that some people think father and son Alain and Philippe Viret are completely bonkers. And why? Well, it's all to do with the fact that they've invented an agricultural system called cosmoculture, inspired by the Inca and Mayan civilizations.

In essence, they believe that they can create positive energies in the vineyard and in the winery by capturing the cosmic forces from the planets and constellations, which, in turn, are transferred to their wines. Techniques in the vineyard include installing cosmic posts to draw in energy and placing stones near sources of natural water

(Alain Viret is a dowser, rather handily) to act as a kind of vineyard acupuncture. As to the winery, this was designed according to the rules of the Golden Number to create a perfect equilibrium – and if this is all beginning to sound distinctly quirky and mystical, you may be comforted to learn that the pyramids and many medieval cathedrals and temples were constructed under these rules.

So are the wines any good? Well, yes, they are, but there is no way of knowing whether this is the direct result of their extraordinary way of going about things. They could just be naturally brilliant winemakers.

LOOK FOR:
▸ Maréotis, light-bodied and very aromatic
▸ Les Colonnades, made from old vines
▸ Emergence, which is the most powerful wine of the estate

Southeast of the city of Avignon, in the department of Vaucluse, lies the picture-postcard pretty district of Côtes du Lubéron, where the vineyards vie for position with fields of lavender and a patchwork of olive, almond and peach orchards. The cool air on the slopes of the Lubéron hills favours the cultivation of white-grape varieties as well as red – indeed, this area produces relatively more white wine than any other of the Rhône. These are fruity to taste, but could never be described as heavyweights. Even the red wines are quite pale and light-bodied because the red grapes don't always ripen properly thanks to that infernal Mistral.

Slightly further north, Côtes du Ventoux is a big, 7700-ha (19,000-acre), largely red-wine district with much potential. It's named after the 1900 metre-high (6250 ft) Mont Ventoux, famous for forming one of the steeper sections of the Tour de France cycle route. Indeed, the best grapes come from vines that clamber as high as 500 metres (1640 ft) up its slopes, giving fresh and fruity wines with a level of acidity that is higher than average by Rhône wine standards.

The most prestigious wine villages of southern Rhône – Châteauneuf-du-Pape, Gigondas, Vacqueyras, Tavel and Lirac – are located a few miles to the north of Avignon and each has its own appellation contrôlée.

Châteauneuf-du-Pape, a town and also one of France's best-known wines, takes its name from the 'new castle of the Pope', constructed in the fourteenth century as a summer residence for the pope (at this time, the papacy was seated in Avignon). Only a wall and a tower of the 'new castle' remain, but the ruins offer a magnificent view over the vineyards, whose owners are entitled to emboss the old papal coat of arms on the neck of their bottles. In style, the wines are powerful and full-bodied with plenty of sweet, succulent summer-fruit flavours that are the direct result of ultra-ripe grapes, ripening that is encouraged by large, smooth pebbles (called 'galets roulés') that litter the vineyards – these collect the heat of the sun during the day and radiate it at night, making these vineyards some of the hottest in France. Incidentally, Châteauneuf-du-Pape was the very first place in the world to introduce a system of vineyard and wine classification designed to combat fraudulent wine imitations – the prototype of today's appellation-contrôlée structure.

CHÂTEAU DE BEAUCASTEL, CHÂTEAUNEUF-DU-PAPE

One of the greatest estates of France, the well-respected Perrin family, headed by Jacques Perrin and run by his sons François and Jean-Pierre, have owned 100 ha (247 acres) of prime grape-growing land – which they farm organically – since the seventeenth century. Here, they cultivate 13 different grape varieties because, uniquely, they use all 13 of the permitted varieties for their red Châteauneuf-du-Pape. Having said that, there is an unusually high percentage of Mourvèdre and Syrah in the blend, giving rich, tannic reds that need to be tucked away for at least a decade before they reach their best.

They produce wine at three different levels: Château de Beaucastel are top-of-the-range wines made from the finest grapes of the oldest vines; those bottled under the Perrin et Fils label offer the next level down in quality, using bought-in fruit and fruit from their own younger vines; La Vieille Ferme is the label used for their reliable, everyday, around-a-fiver wines.

The family is passionate about matching the right wine with the right food to the extent that they even employ a three-star Michelin chef in-house. When they are not eating, Jacques Perrin is busy in his roles as president of both the French Wine Academy and the International Wine Academy.

LOOK FOR:
▸ Cuvée Hommage à Jacques Perrin (made only in exceptional years)
▸ Roussanne Vieilles Vignes
▸ Côtes du Rhône Coudelet de Beaucastel, red and white
▸ Perrin et Fils Vinsobres (note that older vintages of this wine may be labelled Vinsobres-Côtes du Rhône-Villages – the village of Vinsobres was promoted to appellation-contrôlée status only in February 2006)

TASTING NOTES

Tesco Finest Châteauneuf-du-Pape, 2004

Oz says: A 'quite' wine. Quite attractive. Quite full. Quite good. But not exciting.

James says: I've heard of Châteauneuf-du-Pape. This is the sort of wine that makes your teeth feel a bit furry, like rhubarb. 'Neuf' said. No thank you, garçon.

Travelling a little further north brings you into Vacqueyras and Gigondas territory that is situated in the shadow of the pointy, teeth-like Dentelles de Montmirail mountains. These are warm, herby, spicy, Grenache-based red wines brimming with rich mulberry, plum and cherry flavours for the most part – though Gigondas (a name that very aptly comes from *jocunditas*, the Latin for 'joy') is more concentrated in flavour. Both offer excellent value for money.

Incidentally, last summer a group of growers opened a 6-km (4-mile) walking trail through the vineyards of Vacqueyras, with plenty of informative signs along the way (written in English). There are also colour photographs and drawings to give visitors an introduction to viticulture (or what happens to the grapes in the vineyard) and the work of the grape grower.

The southern Rhône is also home to Tavel, France's most famous rosé. Based on Grenache, it is a powerful, but curiously unrefreshing, wine with a slightly orangey colour. Lirac rosé, which is better, is another Grenache-dominated wine. It is still pretty powerful but much fresher and, usually, delicious to drink. The warm, southern climate equals ripe grapes, rich wines and bold flavours. You can expect to taste succulent, juicy red cherries, summer pudding, licks of toffee, hints of black pepper and, sometimes, a sprinkling of herbs or spice – and that's just from the rosés. Always dry in taste, you're tempted to just crack them open and quaff them on hot summer days. But they're strong. You'll end up asleep in the flower bed if you're not careful.

Sparkling Clairette de Die, made from a blend of Clairette and Muscat grape varieties by a method known as méthode Dioise, is a magnificent, outdoor, summery kind of fizz. Off dry and grapey in taste, it's incredibly easy to drink. This comes from the Drôme valley, 40 km (25 miles) east of the Rhône river in the ancient winemaking region of Dioise, which is now counted as part of the Rhône region. The dry Crémant de Die, a traditional-method sparkling wine (see page 121), is also produced here, but this isn't half as tasty as Clairette de Die. Nobody is allowed to say méthode champenoise or champagne method any more because these terms were outlawed in 1994, so look for fizz with terms like

FAT BASTARD WINES
Ten years ago, Rhône winemaker Thierry Boudinaud and UK wine importer Guy Anderson got together to dream up a new blend of wine with which to excite the UK market. On tasting a particularly rich and rounded experimental batch of Chardonnay, Boudinaud exclaimed, 'Now that is what you call a fat-bastard wine' – and the name stuck. The wine isn't sold in the UK any more (simply because these fun-named wines have gone out of fashion), though five million bottles are exported each year to the United States under the Fat Bastard label – the Chardonnay has been joined by wines made from the Syrah, Sauvignon Blanc and Cabernet Sauvignon grape varieties. Strictly speaking, Fat Bastard wines aren't Rhône wines because they are made from grapes grown in the Languedoc-Roussillon region. A large bottling plant was required for this project, however, so the wines are trucked to the Meffre winery at Gigondas for bottling and shipping.

Crémant or Traditional Method on the label instead. Any fizz that emulates the production techniques of champagne described on page 178 – is always going to top notch.

It's pretty straightforward to find these wines in France because any fizz with Crémant in its name will have been made to the highest standards (that is, in the same way as champagne). Crémant d'Alsace and Crémant de Bourgogne are the best known. Blanquette de Limoux from the Languedoc-Roussillon region, plus a couple of Loire-valley sparklers, are also produced via the traditional method.

As for the rest, the transfer method is the next best way of putting the sparkle into wine. The secondary fermentation takes place in bottle, so the wine has the opportunity to absorb some of the yeasty flavours from its lees (the dead yeast cells). However, it is then transferred under pressure to large tanks for filtering, dosage (see page 179) and re-bottling. The end product won't be in the same league as traditional-method wines, but it's much faster – and a lot less expensive – to create.

When the whole of the fizz-making process takes place in tanks, it is described as the Charmat or cuvé-close method. It's a much cheaper way of doing things, but the wine has no complexity because it doesn't get to spend time on its lees and the bubbles will be larger (and therefore the wine will lose its fizz more quickly after opening). Nevertheless, even this technique is heaps better than the continuous method, whereby the wine acquires its (huge) bubbles as it passes through a series of pressurized tanks.

Finally, a handful of French sparklers (for example, Gaillac Mousseux from the southwest of the country) are made using the méthode rurale (also called méthode ancestrale) where the wine is bottled and sealed while it is still undergoing its primary fermentation. These can be cloudy, but that's not a fault, for once. And then there is the méthode Dioise used to make the Rhône valley's Clairette de Die. Here, the fermentation is stopped before all the grape sugar has been used up, that is, the wine has some sweetness to it, and it is then filtered and re-bottled under pressure.

In a different style altogether, the Rhône also produces two Vins Doux Naturels: the terrific, white, grapey Muscat de Beaumes-de-Venise and the not-so-terrific, Grenache-based red Rasteau. The former is truly scrumptious, packed full of rich, sweet, peach, honey, orange peel, apple and grape flavours that simply linger on and on. The pretty village of Beaumes-de-Venise possesses an especially hot climate that helps to promote a super-ripening of the grapes, which in turn means that the juice they contain is ultra-sweet from natural sugars. Vin Doux Nature translates as 'natural sweet wine', but it's not natural at all. In fact, these wines are created by adding grape brandy to partially fermented wine. The heady strength of the spirit (96 per cent alcohol by volume) kills the yeasts and the fermentation stops in its tracks. As a result, the wine still contains unfermented sugar, so it is very sweet to taste and is often high in alcohol (16 to 20 per cent). Some are bottled straightaway to preserve their aromas (any Vin Doux Naturel made from the Muscat grape variety provides the perfect example), while others are aged in oak barrels for a few years before bottling.

Just south of the town of Montélimar, you'll come to the primarily red-wine districts of Côtes du Vivarais to the west of the river Rhône in the Ardèche department and Coteaux du Tricastin and Vinsobres (what a great name) to the east of the river, in the Drôme department. Decent wine pops up in these areas occasionally, but on the whole you won't need to linger here. The best reds – which are often made entirely from the Syrah grape variety – hail from the Coteaux du Tricastin. This is also the source of two-thirds of France's truffle supply. Traditionally, pigs were used to sniff out these highly prized delicacies, but truffle hounds (a sort of poodle–beagle cross) are trained for this purpose nowadays and a good dog can unearth 2 to 3 kg (roughly 4 to 6 lb) of truffles per hour.

The rugged north

You now have to drive about 44 km (27 miles) to reach the north of the region – and what a difference that journey makes. Thanks to the northerly winds, it's much cooler (relatively, anyway) and the landscape has changed dramatically. The river is at its narrowest here, cutting through a rugged, rocky plateau some 350 metres (1148 ft) above the valley floor. There are no swathes of vines; instead, a narrow strip of terraced-vineyard plots clings to the spectacularly steep cliffs that line the river, and these are the source of the stunning (and fabulously pricey) wines of Côte-Rôtie, Hermitage and Condrieu, ranked among the best in the world.

Make your first stop in the village of St-Péray where a small amount of white wine is made (both still and sparkling), from a blend of Marsanne and Roussanne grape varieties. The fizz used to be dull and heavy, but now isn't too bad, and the still wine can be quite tasty, sometimes even a bit perfumed.

The village of Cornas comes next on the road north and this makes red wine only. All northern Rhône reds are based on the Syrah grape variety that flourishes on the granite, schist and gneiss soils. Here, this variety

is at its most powerful, giving dense, warm, tarry wines with heady
aromas and flavours of blackcurrant, raspberries, herbs and chocolate.
This is the wine to buy if you cannot afford Hermitage and Côte-Rôtie
because it shares similar flavours – but not their price tags.

Moving ever northwards, Crozes-Hermitages is the largest
winemaking area of northern Rhône (1280 ha/3162 acres in total)
creating mainly soft, smoky, blackcurranty, full-bodied red wines that
offer great value. The vines are cultivated on the plateau surrounding the
towering, granite hill of Hermitage, famous for the memorable, highly
prized, historic red and white Hermitage wines (vines were being grown
here in Gallo-Roman times). The potent, 100 per cent Syrah reds are
renowned for their ability to age for decades, while the whites, created
from a blend of Marsanne and Roussanne grape varieties, can last as
long as 40 years. To enjoy the very best wines, look for a vineyard name
on the label (such as Les Bessards, Le Méal, Les Gréffieux or Rocoule),
indicating that the grapes used to make it hail from one of the top
vineyards – well, plots more like – on the hill. These single-vineyard
bottlings are rare, so be prepared to pay a king's ransom for them.

M. CHAPOUTIER, HERMITAGE

This long-established though highly progressive
merchant business (see page 156) specializes
in serious yet exciting wines from the northern
Rhône (most especially Hermitage), as well as
Châteauneuf-du-Pape. Since 1987, it has been run
by the dynamic Michel Chapoutier, who has more
vines under biodynamic cultivation (see page xxx)
than anyone else in France. Their domaine wines
(the extremely expensive ones) account for 30 per
cent of production and these are superior to their
merchant wines, though this is not to say that the
latter aren't good. Far from it.

He has also been innovative in overprinting
all his wine labels in Braille and in setting up
the charitable M. Chapoutier Wines and Health
Association that raises awareness of bone-
marrow transplants.

LOOK FOR:
▸ Hermitage la Sizeranne
▸ Hermitage Cuvée de l'Orée (white)
▸ Hermitage les Varonniers (white)
▸ Hermitage le Pavillon
▸ Hermitage le Méal
▸ Hermitage l'Ermite
▸ Hermitages les Gréffieux
▸ Côte-Rôtie La Mordorée
▸ St-Joseph les Granits (white)
▸ Châteauneuf-du-Pape Barbe Rac
▸ Crozes-Hermitage les Varonnières

A word of warning. These are very expensive.

Heading northwards again, the mainly red wines of the St-Joseph appellation vary greatly in style depending on where the grapes used to make them are cultivated. Top wines, rich in blackcurrant flavours, come from grapes grown on south-facing slopes that are sheltered from the cool, northerly winds and where they capture the best of the sunshine. The vineyards extend from around the town of Tournon all the way up to Chavanay, occupying some 900 ha (2223 acres) in total, so plenty of wine is made and therefore they tend to be lower in price. Good news.

As you head even further northwards, don't blink or you might miss Château-Grillet. This estate has been owned by the Neyret-Gachet family since 1840 and, with only 4 ha (9 acres) of vineyards (all planted with the white Viognier grape variety), is one of France's smallest appellations contrôlées. This explains the high price tag: demand for this white wine always outstrips supply. But one has to question why because it's quite a while since it set the wine world on fire.

Next door, Condrieu is another white-wine-only appellation – and what a wine it is. Here, the Viognier grapes, grown on vertiginous slopes cascading down to the river's edge, are turned into sensational wines boasting a heady, musky and floral perfume and unctuous, peachy flavours. Once again, the area is small, so production levels are low and in years when the weather isn't kind, even less wine is made because Viognier vines need exactly the right kind of conditions if they are to provide plenty of grapes (Viognier is a naturally poor yielder anyway, but it's also vulnerable to poor fruit set and rot in cool and wet years, which reduces the yield even further). Some 30 different grape growers make their own wine; the remaining 70 or so sell their grapes to the region's négociants (see page 139). This may sound a lot, but production is tiny and Condrieu is therefore a rare, highly sought after white wine. This is the perfect wine to drink with Rigotte de Condrieu, a soft cheese, which has a subtle, delicate taste of honey and acacia.

French doughnuts aren't as nice as British ones. They taste of goats' cheese.

DOMAINE GEORGES VERNAY, CONDRIEU
Back in the 1950s, the vineyards of Condrieu all but disappeared because they became so uneconomic to work. Even today, every task must be done by hand because the terraces are not wide enough to accommodate any machinery. Furthermore, every few years the soil that has been washed off the slopes by rain must be painstakingly hauled back up to the top of the slopes.

But back to the 1950s. Step in Monsieur Georges Vernay, who doggedly replanted some of the abandoned terraces, refusing to give in to their treacherous slopes, which led to a revival of the appellation. Indeed, many say that 'Monsieur Viognier' was the saviour of Condrieu.

Today, production of this 7-ha (17-acre) estate – now run by his daughter, Christine, and her husband, Paul Amsellem – is split among Condrieu, Côte-Rôtie and St-Joseph.

LOOK FOR:
- Côte-Rôtie Maison Rouge
- Côte-Rôtie Classique
- Côte-Rôtie Blonde du Seigner
- Condrieu Les Chaillées de l'Enfer
- Condrieu Coteaux de Vernon

The journey through the Rhône region ends at the 8-km-long (5-mile), highly scenic, dauntingly steep, sloping strip of the vineyards of Côte-Rôtie – and it's not called the 'roasted slope' for nothing. The schistose soil has an incredible ability to retain heat, which is radiated back up to the vines. These are mostly Syrah, though some Viognier is grown as well because the wine is officially allowed to be made up of a blend of both Syrah and Viognier (as long as they are fermented together) – indeed, this is one of the reasons behind the remarkable character of Côte-Rôtie, because the Viognier adds a wonderful scent of violets to the wine. The very finest wines – the single-vineyard bottlings that fetch the highest prices – come from any one of 72 vineyard sites that have been officially designated as being superior among the 200 ha (494 acres) under vine. You may also occasionally see the words Côte Blonde or Côte Brune on labels, which refers respectively to whether the vineyards lie south or north of the town of Ampuis. The majority of Côte-Rôtie, however, is produced from vines grown in both areas, owned mostly by small-scale growers who either bottle their own wine or sell to one of the major négociants of the region.

Lyon

France's second-largest city (after Paris) claims the title of gastronomic capital of the world – 'the belly of France' is how some of the less respectful describe it. Some declaration, but whether or not you agree with it, there is no doubt that it's a great destination for anyone who loves good food. For a start, there are more than 40 daily food markets across the city, the best held at the Halles de Lyon on cours Lafayette in the Part-Dieu district.

Lyon's very location means that it can draw together many regional specialities – for example, crayfish, pike and trout fished from Alpine streams to the east, Bresse chicken from the north, hare, quail, partridge and woodcock from the Dombes plateau to the northeast, Charolais beef from the northwest, fruit from the Rhône valley to the south … and the list of local cheeses is endless, though Cervelle de Canut, which translates as 'silk weaver's brain' is perhaps the best named. This herby cream cheese was the favourite of the silk weavers who helped make Lyon rich and it's thought that its name derives from the fact that it looks a little like brains when it is squeezed through muslin. Either that, or the silk weavers weren't held in very high regard.

Lyon's farms provide the pork that is transformed into tasty smoked-ham pâtés alongside rosette, the most famous of Lyon sausages, and boudin blanc, a type of black pudding without the blood. Other Lyon specialities include andouillette à la Lyonnaise (tripe sausages served with fried onions – onions are used in virtually every dish here), salade Lyonnaise (made with lamb shanks and chicken livers), saucisson au brioche (a brioche filled with a mixture of sausages, truffles and pistachio nuts) and tablier de sapeur (tripe cooked with parsley and onions, which is then breaded and fried), so named because it looks like the large, leather aprons, or 'tabliers', once worn by French firemen. Strangely, perhaps, macaroni cheese is also a popular dish in Lyon, but this can be explained by the fact that the river Rhône provided the route north from Italy in the days before the railways and motorways existed.

A fun way of eating in Lyon is at one of the city's many family-run bouchons, which are a kind of bistro, very basic in style – think paper

THE RHÔNE VALLEY'S VINS DE PAYS
For simple quaffing styles, the wines from the Vin de Pays areas of Collines Rhodaniennes, Comtéss Rhodaniens, Coteaux de l'Ardèche, Coteaux des Baronnies and Principauté d'Orange can be unusual and interesting simply because the winemakers are able to experiment with grape varieties that are not approved for use in the region's appellation-contrôlée wines (varieties such as Cabernet Sauvignon, Gamay, Merlot and Chardonnay).

tablecloths and no change of cutlery between courses here – and often very tiny in size. You're not likely to be served foie gras and truffles in these establishments; instead, they make good use of very simple, traditional ingredients, such as cockscombs, pigs' and calves' feet, chicken livers, tripe, cardoons, lentils and Swiss chard. The cooking is done mostly by the women of the household who are the spiritual descendants of Mère Brazier, Mère Fillioux, Mère Guy and the other female cooks who were called 'les mères Lyonnaises', which translates as the mothers of Lyon. During the second half of the nineteenth century, these women started life as in-house cooks to many of the large bourgeois families, but left service to open up their own restaurants. Some say that it was this small band of women who shaped the gastronomy of Lyon that is found today.

TASTING NOTES
Côte-Rôtie, Ogier, 2001
Oz says: This is okay, but not exciting. It's a bit thin and dry. There's some nuttiness and a hint of spice.
James says: Is this a type of barbecue attachment? It's another wood preservative or an industrial by-product. I can't really imagine why anyone would walk into a wine shop and buy this at this price. That's three curries *and* the beer.

Food and wine matching

The red wines of the Rhône rejoice in a symphony of powerful, spicy, fruit-filled and complex flavours and even the white wines share their full-bodied, mouth-filling character. It only makes sense, therefore, to partner them with robust and powerful foods – recipes that call for touches of subtlety could otherwise easily be overwhelmed, even if the principal ingredient is a hunk of red meat or game.

Starting with everyday dishes, drink the reds with Tex-Mex, casseroled beef, nut roast, stuffed peppers, liver and bacon, beef curry, chilli con carne, sausages, corned-beef hash, beef stroganoff, spaghetti Bolognese and cottage pie. Top reds, such as Hermitage and Côte-Rôtie, should be reserved for venison, guinea fowl, pigeon, lamb shank and rabbit.

As far as white Rhône wines are concerned, their creamy personality matches creamy chicken or veal dishes and they also stand up well to crab bisque, honey-glazed duck and Vietnamese cuisine.

WHEN TO DRINK THE WINES OF THE RHÔNE VALLEY
▸ Côtes du Rhône, Côtes du Lubéron, Côtes du Ventoux, Coteaux du Tricastin, Côtes du Vivarais, white Châteauneuf-du-Pape and Rhône rosés should be drunk as soon as you buy them
▸ St-Joseph is delicious at one to two years from the vintage date, but top wines can last for ten
▸ Condrieu is ready at one to three years
▸ Top Crozes-Hermitage is good for drinking at two to five years

▸ Vacqueyras can age for three to ten years
▸ Top Côtes du Rhône-Villages and Château-Grillet are best drunk within five to six years
▸ Côte-Rôtie and top Châteauneuf-du-Pape are ready at eight years
▸ Gigondas and Cornas are best at ten years
Red Hermitage will keep for at least a decade, possibly two or three
▸ White Hermitage can live for up to 40 years

James's Le Spam avec beans (Spam 'n' beans)

SERVES TWO

This traditional hangover cure has been handed down for generations and is very popular in the Hammersmith region of England, where it is usually eaten on a Sunday morning before church.

Ingredients: 1 large tin Spam, 2 large tins beans, 2 small chillies, HP brown sauce, no garlic

▸ Chop the chillies into tiny pieces using a knife with a curved blade and a vigorous rocking motion. Discard the stems. Add a few drops of high-quality virgin olive oil or lard to a shallow pan and fry them for two minutes.
▸ While this is going on, open the Spam tin using the ring pull, or key if it's a very old tin. Remove the block of Spam by levering it out with the point of a knife. Next, slice off the aesthetically unsatisfactory curved ends and put them to one side to eat during the cooking process.
▸ Holding the block between the thumb and forefinger, slice downwards at 8mm intervals whilst avoiding the main artery. Do not allow the block of Spam to collapse. Turn it on one end and again slice at 8mm intervals, then rotate through 90 degrees and slice again to make cubes.
▸ Add these to the frying pan and stir frequently, ensuring all faces of the cubes are cooked. At least two of them should turn brown and crunchy.
▸ While this is going on, empty the two tins of beans into a small saucepan and heat to a gentle simmer, remembering that 'a bean boiled is a bean spoiled.' Decant the Spam pieces into the beans pan and fold in with two dollops of the brown sauce to create an even mixture.
▸ Serve immediately, lightly dusted with chopped coriander (optional).

Matching wine and Spam, by Oz

What is Spam? We think it's Specially Processed. We know it's American. We think it's Meat, but we're not sure. And this ambivalence strikes to the very heart of the perfect Spam 'n' beans 'n' wine pairing. James, of course, adds his own signature touches. One of the main disagreements we had was whether to add the beans to the Spam or the Spam to the beans. I've always been a beans to Spam man, believing that the freshly fired Spam can bruise the beans if carelessly added. But all great dishes have their different interpretations.

   In the event, the perfect Spam 'n' beans match was easy to decide upon. Builders'. Milk and two sugars. An alternative would be whatever £2.99 white wine has stood under the bright lights on the shelves of your corner off-licence for longest. It should exhibit an attractive brownish tinge, smell of fish paste, and taste like the dirt between the hooves of a Clydesdale. Spam 'n' beans will make this snorter taste like a £10 Chablis. Unfortunately, Spam 'n' beans will also make a £10 Chablis taste like the dirt from between a Clydesdale's hooves.

CHAPTER 5 **BURGUNDY**

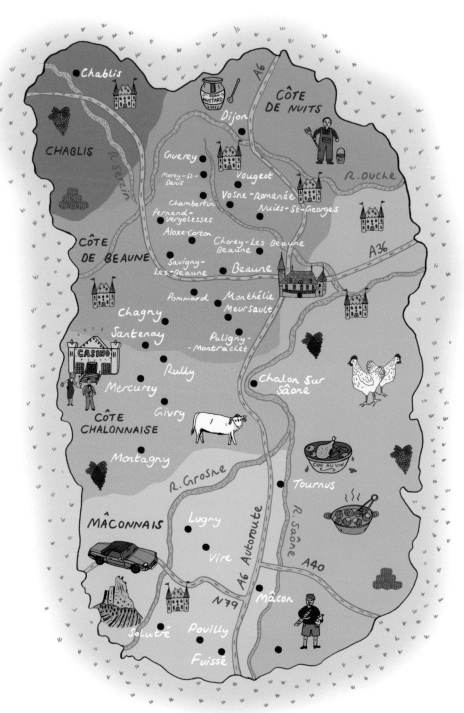

Chablis

CHABLIS

R. Serein

A6

Dijon

DIJON MUSTARD

CÔTE
DE NUITS

R. OUCHE

Gnerey

Morey-St-
Denis

Vougeot

Vosne-Romanée

Chambertin

Nuits-St-Georges

Pernand-
Vergelesses

Aloxe-Corton

Chorey-Les Beaune
Beaune

CÔTE
DE BEAUNE

Savigny-
Les-Beaune

Beaune

A36

Pommard

Monthélie

Meursault

Chagny

Puligny-
-Montrachet

Sartenay

CASINO

Rully

Chalon Sur
Saône

Mercurey

Givry

CÔTE
CHALONNAISE

Montagny

R. Grosne

COQ AU VIN

Tournus

R. Saône

MÂCONNAIS

Lugny

Vire

A6 Autoroute

A40

Solutré

N79

Povilly

Mâcon

Fuissé

To many, Burgundy produces the most sublime wines in the world and it's true that no other wine region can coax the Pinot Noir and Chardonnay grape varieties into performing quite so brilliantly. A somewhat sweeping statement, you might say, but consider this: Burgundy's finest wines are highly sought after and many of them could be sold over and over again, such is their worldwide appeal.

While Burgundy rivals Bordeaux for quality, there couldn't be more differences between the two. Notwithstanding the fact that they grow entirely different grape varieties (and therefore the wines they make are poles apart in style and taste), Bordeaux is all about grand, aristocratic châteaux with all their land whereas Burgundy is a highly fragmented and complicated wine region with many hundreds of separate appellations contrôlées. Owing to complex Napoleonic inheritance laws that divide assets equally among the children of the deceased, there are hundreds of individual vineyard owners with tiny smallholdings (called 'climats'). Furthermore, many different people may own one vineyard and one person or 'domaine' (which is how the Burgundians describe their estates) may own small parcels of land across the region. However, every Burgundian vineyard owner understands every nuance of the soil he or she tills because they insist that the greatness of their wines comes from the soil – indeed, the importance of the terroir of each vineyard is reflected in the way the wines are classified and labelled.

THE ROLE OF THE NÉGOCIANT
A négociant is a type of merchant who buys grapes, grape juice and/or new wine from individual growers and then blends, matures and bottles it before selling it under their own name. Many of the large négociants have substantial vineyard holdings of their own, but nevertheless still need to buy in fruit or wine from smaller growers in order to meet the demands of their order books. It is imperative to stress that while the Burgundians put such great value on the status of the vineyard, the name of the producer tends to count far more in real life.

Top négociants include Bouchard Père et Fils, Duboeuf, Drouhin, Faiveley, V. Girardin, Jadot, Labouré-Roi, Louis Latour, Olivier Leflaive, Maison Leroy, Nicolas Potel, Rodet and Verget.

The grape varieties

Burgundy has been the spiritual home of both Chardonnay and Pinot Noir for centuries and creates wines that everyone wishes to emulate.

The most basic versions of Burgundian Chardonnay are produced in stainless-steel tanks and never see the inside of an oak barrel. Bone dry yet well-rounded to taste, they embrace pure flavours of lemons, crunchy green apples, melons, quinces, greengages, tangerines and peach skin. Top wines, however, are fermented and aged in oak, to give wines with subtle flavours of melted butter, nectarines, pear, honey, quince and figs alongside a creamy, nutty texture.

The fickle Pinot Noir is an incredibly difficult grape variety to grow – and it doesn't always want to ferment. But when it does, it creates gentle, velvety-soft, magical wines, the finest commanding serious money at wine auctions. In youth, they sport the perfume and flavour of ripe damsons, raspberries, strawberries and cherries alongside a hint of spring violets. But as they mellow with age, they develop aromas and flavours of game, prunes, truffles, figs, coffee, chocolate and wet leaves, not to forget the occasional whiff of a farmyard.

Understanding the classifications

The simplest wines are labelled Bourgogne Blanc or Rouge, Bourgogne Grand Ordinaire or Bourgogne Passetoutgrains and can come from anywhere in the region (Bourgogne being what the French call Burgundy). The grapes for these are grown on the most basic soils and an extremely diverse spectrum of wines is produced as a result, though as a rule both reds and whites tend to be light-bodied and fruity in style.

The next level up in quality are the wines called Côte de Nuits-Villages and Côte de Beaune-Villages, which are blends of wine from small groups of villages where the soil is considered slightly superior. An overwhelming amount of Côte de Nuits-Villages and Côte de Beaune-Villages are red. There are also the (again mostly red) wines of Hautes Côtes de Nuits and Hautes Côtes de Beaune that can be quite lean and sharp – the grapes for these are grown on the upper slopes of the hills where it is cooler and therefore the fruit doesn't always ripen to perfection. The best of these are the red Hautes Côtes de Nuits.

Far better-quality wines, however, come from individual villages. Each has their own appellation contrôlée because their soils are considered to be even more superior. Are you keeping up because there's more? The very finest wines are the Premiers Crus (First Growths) and the Grands Crus (Great Growths), named after the vineyards in which the grapes used to make them are grown. And, yes, it is a paradox that the second-best vineyards are called the First Growths. And it gets crazier because it's quite possible for Monsieur X to own a row of Grand Cru vines while the fruit of his neighbour's vineyard, just a stone's throw away, can only be turned into a village wine. But this is how things work in Burgundy – everything really is determined by the quality of the soil, almost stone by stone, crumb by crumb – as you'll discover as you journey through the region. Prepare yourself for an expensive ride, however. Many Burgundies cost two arms and two legs because they're made in tiny quantities, yet everybody wants to buy them.

The Mâconnais

For more reasonably priced wines, start your journey in the south of
the region, in the gently rolling hills of the Mâconnais. Much of its wine
is produced by co-operatives and it has to be said that their everyday
reds and whites (called Mâcon, Mâcon Supérieur and Mâcon-Villages)
are usually somewhat dull – and many are definitely overpriced.
However, the Mâconnais also offers the far superior, creamy, nutty,
fruit-filled white wines of St-Véran and Pouilly-Fuissé. In fact, it's
worth going to Pouilly if only to see the impressive rocks of Solutré
and Vergisson that jut abruptly into the skyline, evoking thoughts
of Hanging Rock in Australia.

While in the area, give yourself time to enjoy a meal in the attractive
town of Tournus, famous for its gastronomy. Regional specialities
include two perennial favourites: coq au vin and boeuf Bourguignon
(though here the latter is taken to a completely different level because
it's made using meat from the local Charolais cattle, claimed to be the
best and most tender beef in France). For something more unusual,
though, why not tuck into gros escargots de Bourgogne (huge snails
that are said to feed on vine leaves, cooked in garlic and parsley butter),
or order pocheuse, a dish first cooked by the bargees on the Saône river
where they caught fish. This filling soup is made with an assortment of
freshwater fish, such as perch, tench, pike, eel and crayfish, which are
browned with bacon and onions, then cooked with herbs, cloves and
wine. It's then flambéed in marc (a spirit distilled from leftover grape
skins and pips) and served with wild mushrooms and garlic croutons.
And, of course, there are the Bresse chickens, famous for their white
feathers, blue legs and red comb – and doesn't it seem a bit odd to think
that a bunch of chooks have had their own appellation contrôlée since
1957?Only the French ...

While you're deciding what to eat, have a glass of the delicious,
biscuity and creamy sparkling Crémant de Bourgogne, most of which
is produced in the Mâconnais. You can drink this straight up or you
can make it even more exciting by dribbling in some Crème de Cassis
(a blackcurrant liqueur from Dijon) to create a Kir Royale.

JEAN-MARIE GUFFENS-HEYNEN

The maverick, trailblazing, outspoken and
flamboyant Jean-Marie Guffens-Heynen first
came to France from his native Belgium to learn
the language – and because he had fallen in love
with French wine. Before long, he and his wife,
Maine, had set up the 3-ha (7-acre) Domaine
Guffens-Heynen in one of the craggiest spots of
the Mâconnais. Ever since the first vintage in 1980,
the wines – all white – have won a reputation for
their high quality and for their fresh, pure and
crisp style, rich in ripe-fruit flavours. Pretty soon,
the demand for Guffens-Heynen wines couldn't
be satisfied, so in 1990 he established a separate
négociant business called Verget and by 2006
he was selling 30,000, 12-bottle cases a year
under the Verget label.

Guffens-Heynen's aim is to make the finest wine
possible – indeed, he is convinced that he makes
the best white wine in Burgundy and doesn't mind
saying so. He is passionate about squeezing every
ounce of expression out of the vineyard, which
he achieves by sourcing grapes only (rather than
unfermented grape juice or wine), drawn from

across the region from small growers with old
vineyards. Something of a perfectionist, he is
extremely choosy about what he buys because
he follows the maxim that top-quality wine can only
be made from top-quality grapes. These are turned
into wine at his state-of-the-art winery in Sologny,
just north of the Pouilly-Fuissé vineyards, where he
has complete control over the winemaking process.

While Guffens-Heynen creates more than 40
different wines, he likes to say that he makes them
in just three styles: wine for when you are thirsty,
wine to make you happy and wine to make you
think. He also believes that wines are like people
and civilizations: they should evolve and change
with time.

LOOK FOR:
- ▸ Verget Mâcon-Uchizy 'La Martine'
- ▸ Domaine Guffens-Heynen Pouilly-Fuissé
- ▸ Domaine Guffens-Heynen Mâcon-Villages
- ▸ Verget Vieilles Vignes de Roally
- ▸ Domaine Guffens-Heynen Mâcon Pierreclos Blanc
- ▸ Verget Pouilly-Vinzelles Les Quarts
- ▸ Verget Pouilly-Vinzelles Levrouté

BURGUNDY

Côte Chalonnaise

Moving northwards into the Côte Chalonnaise, it would be wise to keep a sweater handy because the temperature starts to drop a little. While the area has its fair share of hills dotted here and there, the cold winds from the west waste no time in whipping into the gaps in between. Couple this with the higher elevation of the land and it's no wonder that vineyards can only be found in spots where there is adequate shelter from those wretched westerlies, namely around the villages of Bouzeron, Rully, Mercurey, Givry and Montagny. And what of the wines they produce? Well, the whites (made from either Chardonnay or Aligoté) are generally light-bodied and lemon-sharp in taste, though softer styles of Chardonnay are now emerging from Montagny. The reds, made from Pinot Noir, also lean towards the light-bodied style, the best hailing from Mercurey and Givry (though the latter's whites are also tasty).

It's only a short distance further north to the heart of Burgundy where the vineyards lie snuggled into the leeward side of a limestone escarpment that forms the boundary to the Morvan hills. These vineyards are far less exposed to the wind and, furthermore, are positioned to catch the best of the sunshine.

The Côte d'Or

This is where the vast majority of Burgundy is made and is home to Burgundy's most prestigious vineyards. It comprises a narrow, 50-km (31-mile) ribbon of vines running south–north between Chagny and Dijon, which the locals describe as the Champs-Élysées of Burgundy, and in turn this is divided into the southern Côte de Beaune and the northern Côte de Nuits. Incidentally, if you find yourself in Dijon on a Saturday, check out the Bareuzai food market on rue Musette. It's a great place to try the regional charcuterie, the pain d'épices (a type of gingerbread) and the excellent, creamy and pongy regional cheeses such as Epoisses, Bouton de Culotte and Pierre-qui-Vire.

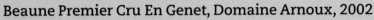

Beaune Premier Cru En Genet, Domaine Arnoux, 2002

Oz says: This is quite gentle and soft. There are mildly smoky strawberries and some rather smoky oak. It's very attractive.

James says: I really like it, though I can't explain why because it's slightly oily and has a gelatinous quality. Leather, that's what it is. It smells like the inside of a Bentley. It tastes as nice as a really old Chesterfield is to sit on.

The Côte de Beaune

Looking at the best of the Côte de Beaune first, make your first stop in Santenay to try the village's good-value red and white wines, perhaps before visiting the historic casino. You never know, you might win, which would be useful in this expensive region. The best Santenay red comes from the Premier Cru les Gravières vineyard, which is not entirely surprising because this lies bang next to the fabulous vineyards of Chassagne-Montrachet. Together with the vineyards of their neighbour, Puligny-Montrachet, the vineyards of Chassagne-Montrachet are responsible for Burgundy's finest Premier and Grand Cru white wines, which reach dizzying heights of quality, longevity – and price. The greatest of all are the Grands Crus of Bâtard-Montrachet, Bienvenues-Bâtard-Montrachet, Chevalier-Montrachet, Corton-Charlemagne, Criôts-Bâtard-Montrachet and Le Montrachet (one of the world's most famous white wines).

Meursault is also another popular wine village (the largest in the Côte d'Or), renowned for creating deliciously rich styles of white wine that are slightly easier on the pocket. Though it has no Grand Cru vineyards, it does have some outstanding Premiers Crus, such as les Perrières, les Charmes and les Genevrières. By the way, this is the perfect wine to drink with a snail soup called soupe d'escargots au Meursault.

148

Vineyard regulations are incredibly specific in Burgundy. The land on the other side of this wall is a valuable vineyard worth millions. Yet on this side of the wall the soil is useless for vineyards and worth nothing.

Moving north towards the town of Beaune, the hillside village of Volnay creates perfumed, stylish, red wines that are generally fairly light-bodied, though richer styles hail from the Premier Cru vineyards of les Santenots and les Champans. For the same flavours at a much lower cost, drive to nearby Monthélie, another hilly village, to try its wines – indeed, only a century ago these wines where actually labelled as Volnay.

Other red wines worth trying before heading into Beaune are the full-bodied Pommard (especially the Premiers Crus of les Rugiens, les Epenots and les Arvelets), the leaner Savigny-lès-Beaunes (in particular the Premiers Crus of les Marconnets, les Narbantons, les Lavières, les Vergelesses, aux Guettes and les Serpentières) and the soft Pernand-Vergelesses (and also taste the attractive white wines of this village). Chorey-lès-Beaune is a forgotten red-wine village making fine, affordable wine in good vintages. And last but by no means least comes the village of Aloxe-Corton, lying beneath the mighty hill of Corton that is home to two Grand Cru vineyards: Corton-Charlemagne (white wine only) and Corton (the only red Grand Cru site in the Côte de Beaune).

TASTING NOTES

Marks & Spencer Chablis, 2004

Oz says: A nice, soft, easy-drinking wine with an apple flavour and gentle hints of earth and minerals. Good, but a little softened. Some vegetable, too. Lettuce leaf?

James says: I honestly can't think of a single thing to say about this wine. I don't like or dislike it. It's a clear liquid.

ALEX GAMBAL, BEAUNE

Born in Washington, DC, Alex Gambal first fell in love with Burgundy in 1993 and established his négociant business just four years later, having learnt in between everything there is to know about grape-growing and winemaking.

He is a great believer in the view that good winemaking, though imperative, comes second to the quality of the grapes and he also has great respect for the character of each appellation and each vintage. His aim is to buy grapes from tiny parcels of vineyards with low-yielding vines and he works closely with the growers to ensure that the highest-possible standards of viticulture are met.

All the wines are made in an artisanal manner, which is to say that it is done in small batches and everything is done by hand. His objective is to produce no more than 60,000 bottles of wine each year (60 per cent white, 40 per cent red), though he doesn't always achieve this. In 2004, for instance, only 36,000 bottles of wine were made.

The high respect earned for his range of wines (which come from up and down the Côte d'Or) is a reflection of his passion for producing fine Burgundy.

Beaune

No trip to Burgundy would be complete without a visit to the charming little town of Beaune, the wine capital of the region. There's plenty to admire – medieval ramparts, a wine museum and the Hôtel-Dieu with its magnificent, glazed tiles in brown, yellow, red and green – and if you haven't emptied your wallet already, you'll find no shortage of wine shops and cellars. One of the most famous sights of the town is the Hospices de Beaune, founded in 1443 by Nicolas Rolin as a charitable hospital. In fact, the Hospices owns a considerable chunk of land in Burgundy (over 60 ha/148 acres) and every November, during a three-day festival called Les Trois Glorieuses, it sells the wine this land provides at a charity wine auction, usually for higher-than-average prices.

Beaune is another good place in which to taste the local food: oeufs en meurette (poached eggs in red wine), rigodon (a baked ham-and-egg custard), le treuffe (boiled potatoes mashed with local cheese and then fried as potato pancakes) and jambon persillé (ham, veal shin and calves' feet cooked in wine, onions, shallots, garlic, cloves and herbs, served cold in its own jelly). And don't forget to buy some Flavigny aniseed balls to take home with you. Until the nineteenth century, it took six months to make the finished product – each seed was rolled in sugar syrup, which had to dry completely before being coated in more sugar syrup. This process was repeated again and again until the sweet had reached the perfect size. Nowadays, 250 tonnes are produced each year.

The Côte de Nuits

The ribbon of vines now snakes its way through the Côte de Nuits, the birthplace of many of Burgundy's most eminent wine names and almost entirely Pinot Noir country. Here, you can follow the winding Route des Grands Crus and taste the wines that under the laws of supply and demand are some of the world's most expensive.

Pause first in Nuits-St-Georges, which has no Grand Cru vineyards but boasts no less than 39 very reliable Premiers Crus. While you are here, take time to visit the Cassissium, a museum dedicated to blackcurrants, the fruit used to make Crème de Cassis and the regional liqueur – indeed, there is even a 40-km-long (25-mile) Blackcurrant Route.

After 45 years, Jean-Pierre's dad felt it was time to take the stabilizers off his bicycle.

Romanée Conti charges up to £1000 a bottle for its red wine and doesn't give a stuff what you think of its shabby old signpost.

Now move on to Vosne-Romanée, considered to be the greatest village of the Côte de Nuits. Not only does it contain 13, top-performing Premier Cru vineyards, but it's home to an incredible five Grands Crus, namely Richebourg, La Tâche, La Romanée, Romanée-St-Vivant and La Romanée-Conti (one of the most expensive wines in the world). These lead into the Grand Cru vineyards of Echézeaux and Grands-Echézeaux, making wines that are revered for their perfume and richness of taste.

A few miles further on takes you to the village of Vougeot, best known for the famous, walled, medieval château of Clos de Vougeot. This striking building (which also houses a wine museum) is set in 50 ha (124 acres) of Grand Cru vineyards that are owned by over 80 different people, so it's worth stating that the quality of the wines depends greatly on exactly where on the estate the grapes were grown and on who has turned them into wine. Look for wines from B. Ambroise, Amiot-Servelle, Chopin-Groffier, J.-J. Confuron, R. Engel, Faiveley, Grivot, Anne Gros,

Haegelen-Jayer, Jadot, Domaine Leroy, Méo-Xamuzet, D. Mortet,
Mugneret-Gibourg, J. Raphet and Vougeraie.

The nearby villages of Chambolle-Musigny and Morey-St-Denis
have a reputation for producing the most perfumed, elegant and delicate
wines of Burgundy. But to guarantee this quality, you must buy their
Grands Crus: Le Musigny, Bonnes-Mares, Clos de la Roche, Clos
St-Denis, Clos de Tart or Clos des Lambrays.

The band of Grand Cru vineyards sweeps into Gevrey-Chambertin,
the largest of the Côte de Nuits wine villages, which flaunts a record
nine. Le Chambertin and Chambertin-Clos de Bèze are the most
celebrated. While you're here, though, make a point of tasting the
outstanding Premier Cru Clos St-Jacques and Premier Cru Combe
aux Moines – these really deserve to be awarded Grand Cru status.

Wines are stored in multiples of 12 in Burgundy. This wine really needs 10 years to age, but clearly the winemaker couldn't wait.

BURGUNDY

Clos Vougeout is the most famous walled vineyard in Burgundy, but the vines down by the road don't make very good wine. Only the ones further up the slope are worth the daunting asking price.

DOMAINE DE LA ROMANÉE-CONTI, CÔTE DE NUITS

You have to ask yourself whether any wine is worth £650 a bottle. But the iconic Romanée-Conti, a red wine from Domaine de la Romanée-Conti (or DRC as it's called in the trade), always fetches this kind of money because only tiny quantities of it are made and it's one of the most sought-after wines in the world. Indeed, the whole of DRC, considered by many to be Burgundy's greatest wine estate, produces a total of only 90,000 bottles a year across its range.

So why are DRC wines so exceptional? Well, for a start this 26-ha (64-acre) estate, co-managed by Aubert de Villaine and Henri-Frédéric Roch, is made up of nothing but platinum-quality Grand Cru vineyards. Five of these – Richebourg, Echézeaux, Grands Echézeaux, Romanée-St-Vivant and Montrachet – are shared with other growers, but they wholly own both Romanée-Conti and La Tâche.

All of the vineyards are farmed organically and if you visit the estate at the right time of year, you may even see the horse and plough that are still used here. All of the vines are old and the wines they make are out of this world. There is something bewitching about them. Put simply, they are quintessential Pinot Noir.

well known for being one of the first proprietors in Burgundy to introduce the practice of biodynamic viticulture. Based on the philosophies of Austrian social philosopher Rudolf Steiner, biodynamic growers are organic, but they take it one step further. For example, the rules with regard to what may be added to the soil and when it is applied are far stricter. Indeed, the timing of all vineyard activity is governed by the natural rhythms of the earth and the phases of the moon. Homeopathy is also practised and, just to give you some idea of what's involved, key applications include boiled horse-tail and horn dung (made by burying a cow's horn filled with dung – and it must be a cow's horn, not a bull's horn, because the former accentuates the 'primordial feminine').

Domaine Leroy owns parcels of vines in nine Grand Cru vineyards (Corton-Charlemagne, Corton-Renardes, Richebourg, Romanée-St-Vivant, Clos de Vougeot, Musigny, Clos de la Roche, Latricières-Chambertin and Chambertin), eight Premier Cru vineyards (in Volnay, Savigny-lès-Beaune, Nuits-St-Georges, Vosne-Romanée, Chambolles-Musigny and Gevrey-Chambertin) and a number of other Côte de Nuits sites (sold under the village appellation). All but Corton-Charlemagne produce red wines.

DOMAINE LEROY, CÔTE DE NUITS

The extrovert, outspoken and dog-loving Madame Lalou Bize-Leroy, one of France's most gifted and brilliant winemakers, has been crafting wines of extraordinary quality for around 50 years – indeed, she claims to have been given her first sip of wine 15 minutes after being born. She established Leroy in the early 1990s, having come from the renowned Domaine de la Romanée-Conti, and there are many who believe that this is now the finer estate of the two (a tough call). But this incredible woman is also

DOMAINE DES BEAUMONT

Thierry Beaumont, fourth-generation winemaker, private pilot and former motorbike champion, is a prime example of the new breed of grower-turned-domaine-owner to emerge in Burgundy over the past 20 years or so. His fruity Gevrey-Chambertin and Morey-St-Denis were previously sold to négociants, but from 1999, this risk-taker has been bottling, selling and marketing his own wines. Look out in particular for his Gevrey Premier Cru Les Cherbaudes.

Chablis

The journey through Burgundy ends at Chablis, roughly two hours' drive north of Beaune. This is a tiny area where Chardonnay (the only grape variety to be grown here) produces one of the world's most illustrious dry white wines.

The vineyards are planted on the slopes that rise from the river Serein in a soil called Kimmeridgian limestone, which gives the wines a flavour that can only be described as steely. To draw a parallel, if you've ever accidentally swallowed even a sliver of tin foil, you will know the taste it leaves behind in your mouth – 'steely' is similar, but far, far more pleasant. In addition, all Chablis share a lively, lip-smacking streak of citrus-fruit acidity, encouraged by the cool, northerly climate.

The simplest, and rawest styles are called Petit Chablis and these come from grapes grown on the flattest land of the district at the top of the slopes where it is coolest. Vines planted on north- and east-facing slopes give the wines labelled as Chablis and they possess a little more personality. The superior Chablis Premier Cru, with its appetizing flavour of nuts and oatmeal, hails from the south- and west-facing slopes that benefit from more sunshine – and there are no fewer than 40 vineyards with this designation, the best being Montée de Tonnerre, Mont de Milieu, Fourchaume and Montmains. The seven, top-class Chablis Grands Crus are outstandingly rich, complex and long-lived, and come from a stretch of hillside opposite the town of Chablis, where there are perfect conditions of soil and climate.

Incidentally, you may be wondering why this area is counted as part of Burgundy. Well, historically, there used to be a contiguous seam of vineyards joining Dijon to Chablis that supplied 'jug' wines to the ever thirsty Parisians, but these were wiped out during the eighteenth century by a ruthless aphid called phylloxera that kills vines by chomping away at their roots. There was little point in replanting these vineyards because, by then, the railways had been built, which meant that far superior wines could be transported into the capital from the south – the market for these very ordinary wines had dried up, in other words.

DOMAINE D'ELISE, CHABLIS
The entertaining Frédéric Prain bought this 13-ha (32-acre) estate in 1982 as a civil engineer who knew absolutely nothing about winemaking. He specializes in Chablis and Petit Chablis, the latter of which can be disappointing in the hands of indifferent winemakers. But Monsieur Prain keeps the grape yields low by vigorous pruning throughout the growing season and harvesting is done as late as possible to ensure a generously fruity wine.

WHEN TO DRINK BURGUNDY
▸ The wines of Mâcon, St-Véran, Rully and Monthélie should be drunk as soon as you buy them
▸ Mercurey, Givry, Montagny and white Pernand-Vergelesses are good at two to four years from the vintage date
▸ Crémant de Bourgogne is ready at one to two years
▸ White Savigny-lès-Beaunes requires two to three years
▸ Chablis Premier Cru and Pouilly-Fuissé are drinkable at anything from two to ten years

▸ Nuits-St-Georges, Santenay and red Savigny-lès-Beaunes need around four to six years
▸ Chassagne-Montrachet, Volnay, red Pernand-▸ Vergelesses and Vosne-Romanée can be drunk at six years, but are better if you leave them for ten
▸ Meursault can age for between five and ten years
▸ Chablis Grand Cru, Pommard and the Grands Crus of Aloxe-Corton, Echézeaux, Vougeot, Chambolle-Musigny, Morey-St-Denis and Gevrey-Chambertin should be cellared for at least ten years
▸ The Grands Crus of Puligny-Montrachet can improve for up to 20 years

Food and wine matching

By definition, oaked whites are complex and full-bodied and are therefore able to cope with richly flavoured fish dishes and the kind of sauces with which they are served. Save the Premier Cru and Grand Cru whites (the pricey ones) for dinner parties, birthdays, wedding anniversaries and other special occasions. Indeed, gravadlax, crayfish, dressed crab, Coquilles St-Jacques, scallops mornay, lobster thermidor, Dover sole, Atlantic salmon cutlets, chargrilled tuna and swordfish steaks all clamour for these classy wines. Basic white Burgundy is highly versatile, though, and can be drunk with any of the following foods: potted shrimps and other seafood-based starters, paella, chargrilled chicken with herbs, macaroni cheese and chicken tikka masala.

Not surprisingly, perhaps, mature red Burgundy, with its farmyardy, gamey aromas, goes well with wild-mushroom risotto and roast pheasant. Serve Emmental and Gruyère cheeses afterwards and you can keep on drinking the same wine.

A warning from the campsite by James

In the olden days, camping was a much more strenuous and challenging activity than it is today. Tents were made of weighty orange canvass that could completely compress the suspension of a MkI Ford Cortina and had to be coated with a foul-smelling waterproofing compound once a year. The tent frame was made of steel girders, the arrangement of which was a challenge to professors of Euclidean geometry everywhere. Sleeping bags were made of nylon, lined with nylon and filled with nylon stuffing. They were bright blue, or brown. Camping was a pretty hideous experience.

Today's tent is very different. It is often green to express our sympathy with the delicate balance of the rural environment, and to ensure it is almost impossible to find in the dark. It is made of a breathable and very strong modern synthetic material which, though incredibly tough, is also thin and light, allowing the whole tent to pack into a the back pocket of a pair of Millets action trousers. Modern camping equipment is a marvel of materials science, industrial design and packaging.

And yet, in so many crucial ways, the ancient craft of 'going camping', the response to some deep-rooted and visceral urge to abandon our brick-built and fully plumbed homes to lie in a field and permit nothing more than a gossamer-thin sheet of fabric to interrupt our commune with the earth, has not altered one bit. Camping is still crap.

This may because many of the external factors governing our enjoyment of camping – the weather, the formation of dew, the presence of arachnids, the flatulence of drunken middle-aged higher primates and the need to urinate in the middle of the night – have not changed for many millions of years, and are not going to simply because some geek in a laboratory has come up with Goretex.

Essentially, camping is damp and smelly. What is advertised as a two to three-man tent is actually a survival device designed for arctic conditions in which two to three men need to share body warmth in order to stay alive. What the shopkeeper called a sleeping bag is actually a type of straightjacket for people who were mad enough to go camping when they could have stayed in Madame de Langoustine's beautiful château on the banks of the Gironde.

The only way to ensure a good night's sleep on a campsite is to abandon dinner and consume instead a magnum of 1990 Château Pichon Baron and several bottles of Château Smith Haute Lafitte. Be aware, though, that this little lot will come to considerably more than the price of the tent.

CHAPTER 6 **FROM ALSACE TO CHAMPAGNE**

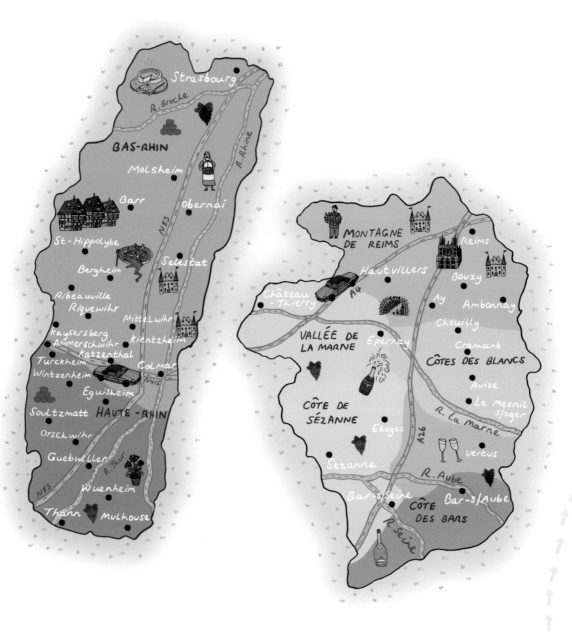

Strasbourg

R.Bruche

BAS-RHIN

Molsheim

Barr   Obernai

St-Hippolybe

Bergheim   Selestat

Ribeauville
Riquewihr

Mittelwihr

Kaysersberg   Kientzheim
Ammerschwihr
Katzenthal
Turckheim   Colmar
Wintzenheim

Eguisheim

Soultzmatt   HAUTE-RHIN

Orschwihr

Guebwiller

R.Thur

Wuenheim

Thann   Mulhouse

R.Rhine

N83

N415

N83

MONTAGNE
DE REIMS   Reims

Hautvillers   Bouzy

Château   Ay   Ambonnay
-Thierry   CAVE
Chouilly

VALLÉE DE   Epernay   Cramant
LA MARNE   CÔTES DES BLANCS

CÔTE DE   Avize
SÉZANNE   Le Mesnil
s/oger

R. La marne

Eboges   Vertus

Sezanne   R. Aube

Bar-s/seine   Bar-s/Aube
CÔTE
DES BARS

R.Seine

A4

A26

It's time to turn up the heating in the car. The roads have headed into the bleak plains of northern France where the climate is distinctly marginal when it comes to grape-growing – it's cold, wet and windy here. But, despite all odds, there are some famous vineyards in these parts, thanks to the interruptions of hills and mountains that break the path of the harsh, nippy, rain-bearing, westerly winds that chase across the plains from the Atlantic. As long as the vines can find the best of the sunshine in a protected spot, they can conjure up some of France's finest wines.

ALSACE

The majority of France's vineyards are situated in really pretty, if not beautiful, parts of the country, but nowhere else is quite as picturesque and enchanting as the region of Alsace, nestled into the northeast corner on the German border. Here, a narrow strip of vineyards some 100-km (62-miles) long lies squeezed between the rugged, forested Vosges mountains that separate Alsace from the rest of France and the river Rhine – indeed, much of the region lies within just a short stretch of the river.

It's a truly wonderful place to visit, especially if you explore the Route des Vins that weaves its way through the quaint, unspoilt medieval towns and villages with their tall, pointed, church steeples. Here, you can stop to admire the bulging, often colourful, half-timbered houses that almost lean across the narrow, cobbled streets and to smell the geraniums that spill from every window box and hanging basket. Best of all, the region is host to no less than 46 wine festivals each year, so you'd be jolly unlucky if you missed out on joining in the fun at one of these. They offer you plenty of opportunities to taste the local wine, perhaps before slipping into one of the region's many Michelin-starred restaurants for lunch or dinner. And once inside, why not order choucroute garnie, one of the region's signature dishes? This is prepared by heaping potatoes, slices of smoked pork loin, onions, juniper berries and any number of different local sausages, hams and bacon, all cooked together in goose fat and local Riesling, on to a bed of sauerkraut (finely sliced, fermented, white cabbage with a distinctive, sour flavour). A word of advice: you need to be ravenous to tackle this because the portions are decidedly daunting.

One of the things you will notice as you travel through the region is the high number of German-sounding village names, not to mention the German-sounding local dialect, so it's worth delving just briefly into history here to explain why. For four centuries, Alsace was passed back and forth between France and Germany like a ping-pong ball, finally being reclaimed by the French at the end of the Second World War. As a result, France and Germany have played an equal role in sculpting the region's culture, language and traditions, creating a dual personality that makes Alsace stand out as very different to the rest of France.

This individuality is also reflected in its wines, most specifically in the way they're labelled – most unusually for French wines, they are named after the grape variety from which they have been made rather than by the name of the village in which the grapes were grown. All are of appellation-contrôlée status and marked by a striking fragrance and pure, concentrated flavours, and most are dry to taste and white – the cool, northerly climate effectively rules out production of deep red wines because black grapes rarely ripen fully here. Having said that, there are some tasty ones, the best hailing from the villages of St-Hippolyte and Turckheim, though be warned that these strawberry and cherry-flavoured wines are usually closer to a rosé wine in colour and in body. These wines are the perfect accompaniment to écrevisses au Pinot Noir – river crayfish cooked in Pinot Noir wine. Or you could drink them with the local game (from pheasant to wild boar), which is traditionally served with noodles or dumplings.

In fact, if it weren't for the Vosges mountains, even white grapes would struggle to ripen, thanks to the chilly climate. The mountains, which run

TASTING NOTES

Gewürztraminer Vendange Tardive, Hugel, 2000

Oz says: Quite rich, sweet, fat and ripe, with some rich fruit. It's pretty powerful and deep.

James says: That's off. It tastes like an old bible. Ughh.

roughly north–south, form a barrier to the westerly winds and all the rain they bring with them. This rain-shadow effect creates a mesoclimate on the lee side of the mountains that is warm, sunny and dry – indeed, this is the second-driest place in France (after Perpignan, way to the south). As long as the vineyards are snuggled into the steep foothills on this leeward side, the grapes will ripen successfully.

Alsace's wine route starts at Marlenheim in the Bas-Rhin area, just to the northwest of Strasbourg. While undoubtedly very pretty, if you want to explore the best wine villages of the region, you should head down to the Haut-Rhin area that forms the southern half of the region, because this is where the mountains offer the greatest protection from the prevailing weather blown in from the Atlantic. The best villages to stop at are Bergheim, Ribeauvillé, Riquewihr, Mittelwihr, Kaysersberg, Ammerschwihr (which is home to the oldest and most famous Grand Cru vineyard of Kaefferkopf), Katzenthal, Turckheim, Wintzenheim, Eguisheim (a stunning walled village that lies at the highest point on the wine route), Soultzmatt, Orschwihr, Guebwiller, Wuenheim and Thann.

If you're still hungry, try some of the region's other specialities, such as escargots en brioche. Every region of France prepares snails in its own way and here the snails are cooked, taken from their shell and baked briefly on slices of brioche covered with garlic butter. It's also impossible to resist the delightful Alsatian sweet pastries and cakes. Kugelhopf, a light yeast cake with raisins and almonds that is baked in a special fluted and twisted mould, is a particular favourite of the locals.

Reading the label

Alsace wine labels are incredibly easy to understand on the whole. Alsace AC or Vin d'Alsace AC is the appellation for dry wines made from a single grape variety and the label will always exhibit a grape name – Riesling d'Alsace, for example. The only varieties permitted are Gewürztraminer, Muscat Blanc à Petits Grains (usually shortened to Muscat), Pinot Gris, Pinot Noir, Riesling, Sylvaner and the rare Klevener de Heiligenstein (a name that just trips off the tongue).

Gewürztraminer, Muscat, Pinot Gris and Riesling are the finest grape varieties of the region and when they are grown in the very best pockets of land, the wine they make can be labelled Grand Cru. The Grand Cru areas (50 at the last count) are made up of a collection of top vineyards and when the wine has been produced from fruit grown in just one of these, the label will very often include the name of the vineyard as well. Most of these vineyards can be found on the very steepest slopes of the Vosges foothills and produce exquisite wines.

Vendange Tardive is created from very ripe, late-harvested grapes, yielding rich, mouthfilling wines packed with taste. Once again, only Gewürztraminer, Muscat, Pinot Gris and Riesling qualify. The sweeter, far more intensely-flavoured Sélection de Grains Nobles is made in years when these same late-harvested grapes have been attacked by 'noble rot' (see page 56). If the grapes for either of these styles come from one of the Grand Cru sites, then they can also put this on the label.

Crémant d'Alsace is the region's sparkling wine, made in the same way as champagne. Most are created from the Pinot Blanc grape variety, though other varieties may be used. Incidentally, Crémant d'Alsace is the best-selling sparkling wine in France after champagne.

The majority of Alsace wines are made from a single variety, but wine labelled Edelzwicker is a dry white blend of two or more varieties. Most are based on Sylvaner and Pinot Blanc. Gentil is another blended wine, this time containing at least 50 per cent of Gewürztraminer, Muscat, Pinot Gris or Riesling. Moelleux is a term describes wines that are medium-dry in taste.

Key grapes, key wines

Gewürztraminer is more closely associated with German wines, but it's one of the best grape varieties of Alsace and there's nothing shy about its character. It gives pungent, spicy, luscious wines bursting with the enticing smells and flavours of gingerbread, tea-rose petals, jasmine, sweet peas, lychees, mangoes and Fry's Turkish Delight. These are usually dry, but sweet Gewürztraminer Vendange Tardive and Sélection de Grains Nobles is sometimes made in top vintages, when it takes on exuberant aromas and flavours of honey, dried apricots and exotic oriental fruit. Top Gewürztraminer is made in the villages of Bergheim, Riquewihr, Kaysersberg, Ammerschwihr, Eguisheim, Soultzmatt, Guebwiller and Wuenheim.

Incidentally, Gewürztraminer d'Alsace is the classic, time-honoured partner to Münster, the famously smelly Alsatian cheese that is traditionally eaten with jacket potatoes and finely chopped onions, or with a small dish of caraway seeds. This semi-soft, creamy-textured, tangy cheese was invented in the nineteenth century by the Benedictine monks of the neighbourhood as a way of conserving the surplus milk provided by their Vosgienne cows.

Muscat really smells and tastes of grapes themselves – crunchy green ones, to be precise. Two guises of Muscat appear here – either fragrant, delicate and dry styles, or the rich, sweet Vendange Tardive and Sélection de Grains Nobles that are all syrup, honey, elderflower, rose petal and orange marmalade. These sweet wines are perfect with the local pâté de foie gras – rich, sweet whites are the ideal matches to rich pâtés. The best come from the village of Eguisheim.

Pinot Gris as a dry wine boasts delicious ripe-peach aromas and flavours balanced beautifully by musky spices and just a whiff of smoke. But the Vendange Tardive and Sélection de Grains Nobles made from this grape variety can be memorable – incredibly mellow, with flavours of apricots, raisins, Brazil nuts, honey and treacle, especially if you allow it to age. Top Pinot Gris is made in the villages of Turckheim, Wintzenheim, Orschwihr, Guebwiller and Thann. Dry Pinot Gris wines are powerful enough to cope with bäckeoffe, a tasty hotpot of lamb, beef and pork

marinated and cooked in wine, which originated as a peasant dish. Bäckeoffe means 'baker's oven' – the hotpot would be taken to the baker early in the morning to be cooked while the women went off to the washplace.

Riesling is the most widely planted grape variety in Alsace (and, yes, there's that Germanic influence again because this is yet another German grape variety). Dry styles taste of unripe apples streaked with freshly squeezed lime juice, but as they age they develop fabulous aromas and flavours of baked apple, honey, nuts, butter and, sometimes, a suggestion of petrol (which is actually more appealing than it may sound). Top Riesling is made in the villages of Ribeauvillé, Riquewihr, Mittelwihr, Ammerschwihr, Katzenthal, Eguisheim, Guebwiller and Wuenheim. Drink it with flammekueche, a kind of very flat flan made from bread dough topped with crème fraiche, onions and bacon. It is so wafer-thin, in fact, that it's often described as Alsace's answer to pizza. Indeed, flammekueche translates as 'baked in the flames' and dates back to the times when farmers' wives would roll out a thin piece of bread dough to test the heat of their wood-fire ovens before baking their loaves.

Riesling is also used to make cuisses de grenouilles au Riesling, which is frogs' legs cooked in butter, shallots, cream, egg yolk and, of course, Riesling wine. Look out, too, for frog soup – frogs have been eaten in Alsace since the thirteenth century and the city of Strasbourg used to have a frog market next to the fish market.

Food and wine matching

Alsace whites are the perfect wines to drink with the fragrant and spicy cuisines of the Far East. If you're eating very hot curries, you can't go wrong by partnering them with a spicy Alsace Gewürztraminer or an aromatic Alsace Muscat. For milder fare, such as chicken korma, grilled Thai-style prawns, chicken with lime and coriander, Peking duck and chicken with cashew nuts, go for a Riesling.

Looking at Western foods, Alsace Sylvaner is great with pork dishes, while the more delicate Pinot Blanc is wonderful with onion tart and quiches. Choose Riesling for seafood, grilled fish and goat's cheese. Talking of cheese, it's already been said that Gewürztraminer and Münster cheese is a match made in heaven, but this wine is also good with Roquefort, Brillat-Savarin and Epoisses cheeses.

The fuller-bodied Alsace Pinot Gris has a touch of sweetness about it that negates the slight bitterness of chicken livers, so it's one of the best wines to drink with creamy chicken liver pâté. Actually, it's a pretty good choice for any rich pâté. It's also marvellous with poultry dishes such as chicken risotto. Finally, let's not forget Alsace Pinot Noir, which is lovely with roasts of all kinds.

DOMAINE ZIND-HUMBRECHT, TURCKHEIM

One of the most famous names in Alsace, this family-run estate owns some of the finest vineyards in four of the Grand Cru sites (Rangen, Goldert, Hengst and Brand), from which they craft superb, ultra-rich, memorable wines out of Riesling, Gewürztraminer, Pinot Gris and Muscat. Olivier Humbrecht, a former scientist and engineer who is considered to be one of France's finest winemakers, makes these. He was also the first in France to become a Master of Wine and is now the leading light in introducing biodynamic practices (see page 156) to Alsace because he believes firmly in letting the grapes and the soil in which they are grown speak for themselves.

His father, Léonard Humbrecht, was also something of a pioneer. Back in the 1970s, he was responsible for replanting the terraced Rangen vineyards in the village of Thann that had long been abandoned owing to their exceptionally steep gradient, which made them incredibly difficult to cultivate. They still are, in fact. The quality and the sheer power of these wines makes them some of the finest in Alsace.

LOOK FOR:

▸ Zind-Humbrecht wines bearing the names of specific vineyards, such as Clos Windsbuhl, Clos Jebsal, Rangen or Clos St-Urbain
▸ Gewürztraminer Grand Cru Hengst
▸ Muscat Herrenweg de Turckheim
▸ Brand Riesling
▸ Vendange Tardive Goldert

DOMAINE WEINBACH, KAYSERSBERG

Colette Faller and her daughters, Laurence and Cathérine, make some of Alsace's most exceptional and age-worthy wines at their 27-ha (67-acre) estate on the precipitous, terraced slopes surrounding Kaysersberg. They are constantly striving for perfection and have an unrelenting commitment to delivering excellence – indeed, 'Excellence is our motto' is their stated philosophy.

Since 1998, a third of their vineyards have been farmed biodynamically. This was exactly 100 years after the estate was acquired by the Faller brothers, although the property is known to date back to 890 when Empress Richarde gave it to the Abbey of Etival after which it became the Capuchin monastery. Domaine Weinbach, named after the 'wine brook' that meanders through the estate, was established in 1612 by the Capuchin monks.

The domaine sits at the foot of the majestic Schlossberg hill, which protects the vines from cold winds. Furthermore, its stony soils warm up quickly and the reflected heat helps to promote the ripening of the grapes. All of the traditional Alsace grape varieties are cultivated.

LOOK FOR:

▸ Wines labelled Théo, named after Madame Faller's late husband, which are the lightest wines in the range
▸ The gently sweet, late-harvest wines bearing the Ste-Cathérine label, which come from the Grand Cru vineyard of Schlossberg
▸ Cuvée Laurence wines, made from grapes grown in the non-Cru Altenbourg vineyard (most especially Pinot Gris and Gewürztraminer)
▸ Ste-Cathérine Riesling Grand Cru Schlossberg L'Inédit, the top dry white
▸ Quintessence, a Sélection de Grains Nobles created from either Pinot Gris or Gewürztraminer The highly aromatic and powerful Gewürztraminer Grand Cru Furstentum
▸ The Clos des Capucins range, including Sylvaner Réserve, Muscat Réserve and Pinot Noir Réserve

CHAMPAGNE

'I drink it when I'm happy and when I'm sad. Sometimes I drink it when
I'm alone. When I have company I consider it obligatory. I trifle with it
if I'm not hungry and drink it when I am. Otherwise I never touch it –
unless I'm thirsty.'

These words, written by Madame Lily Bollinger in the mid-twentieth
century, encapsulate the very essence of champagne. You can sip it
anywhere at any time with no excuse needed; yet celebrations must have
it. Sometimes it doesn't always matter who made it, just as long as it is
there. While there are plenty of splendid look-alikes around the world,
there is nothing quite as convincing as the real thing; no other sparkling
wine holds such a powerful, magical allure.

First of all, Champagne is a region, found northeast of Paris, as
well as the wine from the region. No other region's wine can call itself
champagne. Unlike the majority of French wine regions, the champagne
story is not about individual villages or vineyards doing different things.
While the vineyards are classified into the good and the not so good, the
source almost never appears on the label because most champagne
is made with grapes drawn from across the region. Instead, it is brand
building that is important and this is controlled by large companies
called merchant houses (also known as négociants-manipulants). These
are the names that you'll recognize, such as Moët & Chandon, Mumm
and Bollinger. Most of these are based in either Reims or Epernay and
many are open to visitors, offering tours of their cellars and, of course,
tastings – an opportunity not to be missed if you're visiting the region.

The merchant houses, together with the co-operatives, are
responsible for 80 per cent of production (300 million bottles each year),
the balance being provided by individual growers who earn their living
by making their own wine rather than by selling their grapes to the big
boys (these will have the words 'récoltants-manipulants', or RM, on
label). Indeed, the latter is heavily dependent on the grape growers –
all 15,000 of them – because they don't possess huge vineyard holdings
of their own, on the whole.

Dom Perignon: famous for inventing the champagne method of making wine sparkle. Actually pipped to the post by our very own Christopher Merrett in London a few years earlier. (They didn't invent the Croque Monsier either).

Talking of grapes, only three varieties are permitted for champagne: the white Chardonnay and the red Pinot Noir and Pinot Meunier. These would be unlikely to survive here given the climate – the annual average temperature in Champagne, France's most northerly wine-producing region, is a chilly 10.5 °C (51 °F) – but two factors make viticulture possible: firstly, the hills and valleys in which the vineyards are planted afford some protection from the worst of the cold, damp westerlies; secondly, the chalky soils of the region not only retain and reflect crucial heat but also have the ability to supply the roots of the vines with just the right amount of water and nourishment in any kind of weather, wet or dry.

While Champagne doesn't make such a fuss about sense of place as other French winemaking regions do, the region is nevertheless divided into five areas recognized as being better for growing one grape variety or another, though to repeat, this kind of information is not given on the label. Pinot Noir flourishes in the Montagne de Reims and the Côte des Bar (in the far south); Chardonnay dominates the Côte des Blancs and the Côte de Sézanne; the Vallée de la Marne best supports Pinot Meunier. Furthermore, each wine village is classified according to the quality of the grapes it grows, with the top performing earning the status of either Grand Cru (the finest) or Premier Cru (the second best). These are really only relevant to the very finest champagnes, which are allowed to append either Grand Cru or Premier Cru to their name.

176

TASTING NOTES

Waitrose Blanc de Blancs Champagne

Oz says: An uplifting, creamy and soft champagne made entirely from Chardonnay. It foams rather than fizzes and I love its cedarwod perfume.

James says: It's no good. I just can't get on with this. I don't even like lager because it's fizzy.

DOM PERIGNON
1638 - 1715
CELLERIER DE L'ABBAYE D'HAUTVILLERS
DONT LE CLOITRE ET LES GRANDS VIGNOBLES
SONT LA PROPRIETE DE LA MAISON
MOËT & CHANDON

The making of champagne

Because of the low temperatures of the region, the grapes usually fail to ripen properly and are therefore low in sugar and high in natural acids at the time of picking. This is OK, though, since good sparkling wine needs to start off life as a high-acid wine. It is nature's magic that turns this tart, undrinkable base wine into extremely moreish fizz.

First of all, a still wine is fermented and blended in the normal fashion (see page 15–16). For non-vintage champagne, however, this is not quite as straightforward as it may sound. Consistency of taste is critical to the big champagne houses and the best of them go to extraordinary lengths to ensure uniformity of style by fermenting the harvest of each grape variety from each vineyard separately. This can often mean that as many as 100 different wines are produced, but these provide the master blender – a highly skilled person – with a wide range of base wines with which to work.

The thin, horribly acidic base wine is then bottled along with a mixture of sugar, yeast and wine (called the 'liqueur de tirage') and is sealed with a crown cap (just like the crinkly-edged metal top that is used to seal beer bottles). As the sugar and yeast interact with each other, a secondary fermentation occurs that creates a little more alcohol but a great deal of carbon dioxide, which is trapped inside the bottle. Luckily, it's a very soluble gas and it dissolves in the wine, creating enormous pressure inside the bottle. It is this gas that generates all of those tiny, tongue-tingling bubbles (often described as the wine's mousse) – the smaller the bubble, the better the quality.

As the yeast cells die and sink to the bottom of the bottle, a gungy deposit or 'lees' form, on which the wine rests for anything from 15 months to several years. This is important because the yeast has a strong creamy flavour and the longer the wine is in contact with the dead yeast cells, the more complex and flavoursome the finished wine will be. Keeping stock tied up like this is costly, though, so as you might expect, only the very best champagne houses allow their wines to spend more than the minimum time allowed on their lees. Vintage champagne and prestige blends (the very top styles) always spend a decent time on the lees.

Nobody wants to drink cloudy champagne, so the next trick is to take the wine off its lees without losing any of those precious bubbles. This is achieved via a practice known as 'remuage' or riddling. Each day for anything up to eight weeks, the bottle is gradually tilted and its contents gently shaken until it has been turned on its head, causing the sediment to slide slowly into its neck. Traditionally, the remuage was done by hand (just one person could turn up to 40,000 bottles per day), though mechanization of this task has now become the norm.

Next, the neck of the bottle is frozen, the crown cap is whipped off and the plug of frozen silt shoots out under the pressure of the dissolved carbon dioxide, a process known as 'dégorgement'. The wine is topped up with a solution of wine and sugar (called the dosage), the sweetness of which depends on the style of wine required.

179

The different styles

Non-vintage champagne is a blend of wine from two or more vintages. The big champagne houses tend to ensure that the taste of this wine doesn't vary from blend to blend and each will have its own house style. Some NVs (as they are often called) are better than others, depending on who has made it and how long it has been aged on its lees. Most NVs are pretty dry to taste, indicated by the word Brut on the label.

Vintage champagne – sometimes labelled Cuvée Millésime – is made from grapes harvested in the year stated on the label and the wine must have been aged on its lees for at least three years. These wines are only produced in top years and are more complex compared with NVs.

Blanc de Blancs is made solely from the white Chardonnay grape variety and is generally delicate and creamy.

Blanc de Noirs, the fruitiest of all champagnes, is made solely from the red Pinot Noir and/or Pinot Meunier grape varieties (though the wine is white in colour).

Rosé champagne ideally boasts a wonderful perfume of cherries and raspberries. They are produced by either allowing some of the colour from black-grape skins to leach into the grape juice before it is fermented, or, more commonly, by stirring a small amount of still red wine into white champagne.

Demi-sec is a sweeter style of champagne.

Cuvée de prestige is the most luxurious style of the lot and is invariably expensive. Frankly, you sometimes wonder whether you are paying for the silly bottle as much as for superior wine. Ideally, you get the very best flavours that the Champagne region can offer. These wines are created from the region's finest grapes from Grand Cru and Premier Cru vineyards and the wines should be matured on their lees for several years before release to give them extra finesse and flavour. Examples include Dom Pérignon (made by Moët & Chandon), La Grande Dame (from Veuve Clicquot), Cristal (from Roederer) and all (yes, all) of Krug's champagnes.

Champage skittles was a popular, if expensive, pastime among the aristocracy.

Comte Audoin de Dampierre's champagne is selling very well. At this rate he'll be able to afford a new car soon.

THE STORY OF A HUMBLE, SEVENTEENTH-CENTURY MONK

Dom Pierre Pérignon, a Benedictine monk of the Abbey of Hautvillers near Epernay, has long been credited as the inventor of champagne as we know it today. The Abbey owned a number of vineyards and Dom Pérignon was a cellarer (the winemaker, in modern parlance) of some considerable skill. He perfected the art of blending different wines and, at first, did all he could to stop them turning fizzy, which they had a natural tendency to do. It was only after he had introduced the use of cork to seal the bottle that the true potential of secondary fermentation was recognized. Most of the abbey fell into ruins at the time of the French Revolution; the Moët & Chandon family bought what remained at the beginning of the nineteenth century.

CHAMPAGNE POMMERY, REIMS

Madame Jeanne Alexandrine Louise Pommery took over the running of the family business when her husband died in 1858. Before long, she had opened an agency in London and during her travels in Britain fell in love with the Gothic architecture. So when she needed to build new premises in her home town of Reims, she modelled them on her new-found, favourite architectural style: a weird but wonderful hotchpotch of towers, spires and domes constructed of brick and stone, completely out of keeping with neighbourhood.

She also bought 60 ha (148 acres) of the hillside of Butte St-Niçaise, just outside of Reims, which included 120 Gallo-Roman crayères or chalk caves that were used to store perishable food (or so it is believed). Madame Pommery converted these into what some people have described as the eighth wonder of the world: a labyrinth of 19 km (12 miles) of tunnels and galleries supported by Norman and Gothic arches, their walls decorated with pictures carved out of the chalk in bas-relief form. You can still visit these magnificent cellars today.

COMTE AUDOIN DE DAMPIERRE

You may never have heard of this charming and charismatic man, a living representative of ancient French aristocracy, and you may never have heard of the champagnes he makes, though you can buy his wine at Harrods, which speaks untold volumes in itself (they sell only the finest, of course). But the quality of his wine is considered to be superb, a tribute to his decision to use grapes from only Premier Cru and Grand Cru villages.

Comte Audoin flaunts a great sense of family and regional history, and looking at the background of the Dampierre lineage, one can understand why. In 1300, the jurisdiction of his ancestor, Guy de Dampierre, count of Flanders and governor of Champagne, stretched from Bruges to Reims (at that time a royal city). By the end of the nineteenth century, the Dampierres had become masters at creating the local sparkling wine. The interventions of two world wars, however, brought production to a halt and Champagne Dampierre disappeared. It became the mission of Comte Audoin to revive the traditional family business and what he has achieved in just 25 years has been nothing short of a miracle within such a highly competitive industry.

The Count also enjoys an enormous passion for cars, more than ever for his five Aston Martins, which he likes to compare to his champagne: 'A quality product'. He used to own ten of them, but was forced to sell half of his collection to pay for his château.

LOOK FOR:
▸ Brut Grande Cuvée, the 'everyday' wine
▸ Cuvée des Ambassadeurs Brut Premier Cru, a 50/50 blend of Chardonnay and Pinot Noir fruit from Premier Cru villages
▸ Grand Cru Blanc de Blancs
▸ Brut Rosé Oeil de Perdrix, a blend of Chardonnay Grand Cru and local red wine
▸ Brut Grand Vintage, a Pinot Noir-led blend, aged for a minimum of six years before release
▸ Vintage Family Reserve Grand Cru, a blend of the best three villages of the Côte des Blancs
▸ The age-worthy Prestige Cuvée Grand Cru, the finest of Dampierre champagnes

Food and wine matching

The Champenoise, who have no regional cuisine to claim as their own, believe fervently that champagne can be drunk at any time and with anything – and because they promote the 'luxury' image, they seem to eat an amazing amount of foie gras in Champagne. As such, they're absolutely happy to drink it throughout the meal, regardless of what is on their plate. And one can see why: champagne doesn't boast a really strong taste, after all, and its gentle acidity – and the bubbles themselves for that matter – mean that any flavour that is there doesn't coat the mouth and fight with the taste of the food.

Having said this, it is worth taking the trouble to match the various styles of champagne to the foods with which they go best. For example, when it comes to starters and snacks, a dry, white, non-vintage champagne is a terrific accompaniment to dim sum, sushi, pheasant terrine and scrambled eggs run through with strips of smoked salmon, while pink champagne works particularly well with prawn cocktail and other shellfish appetizers.

Turning to main courses, a non-vintage style is good with kedgeree, soufflé, chicken in creamy sauces, paella, roast quail, cold game pie and tandoori chicken. Chinese food, however, calls for wines with a smack of sweetness – a demi-sec version is a perfect choice, therefore. If you're eating oysters, wash them down with a champagne Blanc de Blancs; but if it's scallops, crab or lobster – or even caviare – then only vintage champagne will do.

WHEN TO DRINK THE WINES OF NORTHERN FRANCE
▸ Rosé champagne should be drunk as soon as you buy it
▸ Non-vintage champagne benefits from being tucked away for six months
▸ Mid-priced Alsace whites keep for between three and five years from the vintage date
▸ Alsace Grand Cru Vendanges Tardives, Alsace Sélection de Grains Nobles and vintage champagne need at least ten years in bottle before they reach their zenith

Champagne by Oz

I never thought it would be easy to introduce James to the joys of Champagne. He spent most of our trip beating his chest in righteous indignation about the fact that the only thing France seemed to be any good at was providing toffs to produce wines that would please toffs and which would sell for nearer to a hundred pounds a bottle than a fiver. And I got it in the neck too because it was my posh friends who were making this stuff.

Well, OK. But I was trying to give James a bit of a treat, which was rather like trying to give a Rottweiller a playful chuck under the chin. Except that as our trip wound on, he began, unerringly to favour wines that would never see the neon glare of a supermarket shelf. As soon as he'd downed a couple of glasses of my posh friends' pricey grog, this grumpy class warrior was transformed into a poet, a philosopher, and as more and more posh wine surged past his tonsils, through the thick haze of alcoholic delight, I thought I could detect a slurred but heartfelt plaint that I'd ruined him for ever: 'But one more draught of posh wine, please,' before he staggered off to bed, totally seduced by toffs' hospitality, later to wake and crossly recover his egalitarian principles.

Egalitarian principles, my eye. Well, I had just the place for him. Champagne. The home of hype. A place where no-one thought badly of you for being too expensive, but you could end up very short of friends if you sold your wine too cheap. And, of course, he hated champagne. He would, wouldn't he?

The thing is, Champagne is supposed to be expensive. You don't buy it because it's cheap, you buy it because it's not cheap. You don't serve it and crow about how little it cost, you offer it because you want to appear expansive, generous, successful, indulgent and attractive. For the large companies, the positioning and price of a label matters more to many of them than how the wine tastes – they can manipulate price and desirability by throwing heroic amounts of money around. But at the other end of the scale every village in the region has small individual producers who do have to care about how the wine tastes because their trade is largely with visitors and tourists.

And did James appreciate any of this? I wouldn't say he's a champagne convert – he's too fundamentally anti-bubbles; it's not down to earth enough for him. But don't tell his petrolhead friends – he actually bought a box of the stuff from a guy called Pierre Boever (naturally a small artisan producer who made the stuff in his garage and wore dungarees). James may have been seduced by many of my posh friends and their wines, but in Champagne he stayed true to his principles. Sort of.

CHAPTER 7 **MORE PLACES TO VISIT**

Reims

Paris

LOIRE VALLEY

R. Loir

R. Loire

Nantes   Angers   Tours

Dijon

R. Saône

JURA

BEAUJOLAIS

L'Étoile

La Rochelle

SAVOIE

ATLANTIC
OCEAN

R. Dordogne

Villefranche
-sur-Saône

R. Rhône

Bordeaux   Bergerac

R. Garonne

Montbazillac

Cahors

CAHORS

Avignon

BUZET

SOUTH WEST

Montpellier

Marseille

MADIRAN

Gaillac

GAILLAC

JURANÇON

MEDITERRANEAN
SEA

Bastia

CORSICA

Ajaccio

France is a pretty big place. It takes 11 hours to drive from Nantes in the west to Arbois in the east and even a Jaguar XJS couldn't make the journey from northerly Lille to southerly Perpignan in less than 12 hours. All this assumes travelling across the country in the straightest lines possible (not at all feasible in reality, of course). So, yes, France certainly is a pretty big place and there are therefore myriad wine-producing areas that haven't been covered thus far. If you want to explore the rest of France and its wines, this is the chapter that will take you to the best of those missing pieces. Many are individual wine towns or villages. Some are regions or districts. There's even a whole island.

THE LOIRE VALLEY

France's longest river, the Loire, is one of its most enthralling when it comes to wine. Rising in the Massif Central, it charges northwards through the heart of France before slowing down to twist west, finally slipping languorously into the Bay of Biscay at St-Nazaire. In total, it flows for over 1000 km (625 miles) and its sheer length, the subtle differences in mesoclimate (the region is classed as cool over all), the changing landscape and a deep heritage of different winemaking traditions along the way combine to influence the grape variety planted and the style of wine made. And every style of wine is made, embracing famous names and forgotten gems alike, some to be drunk as young and fresh as possible, others needing 20 years to mature.

With such a wealth of diversity, you might expect us to be guzzling gallons of the stuff, but Loire wines have become strangely unfashionable over the years. It seems hard to believe that we once preferred the wines

191

of Anjou to those of Bordeaux, albeit in the Middle Ages when our kings were the counts of Anjou.

Nowadays, it is the Parisians who embrace Loire wines with gusto, a legacy from the days when the Valois kings escaped the capital each summer, erecting as their retreats a chain of romantic and imposing Renaissance châteaux for which the valley is so renowned. As the story goes, the rich pickings of the forest hunts led to a taste for the local wines that apparently went so well with their catch. Hmm. Given their easy-drinking nature, Loire wines are unquestionably food-friendly, but apart from a powerful, mature Bourgueil or Chinon, perhaps, the idea of matching refreshing and light-bodied wines with game demands a huge leap of imagination. By the way, game is still plentiful in the forests that lie between the Loire and the Cher rivers and the cuisine around these parts abounds with rabbit stews, civet de lièvre (a kind of jugged hare) and all manner of dishes containing pheasant. A good one to try is potage St-Hubert, a soup made from pheasant and green lentils.

Today, the Loire valley is the third-largest producer of AC wines in France (behind Bordeaux and the Rhône valley) from over 50,000 ha (123,500 acres) of vines cultivated by some 13,000 small, family-run estates. Roughly half of its wines are white, a quarter red, with the balance being made up of rosé and sparkling wines.

Convention divides the Loire into four viticultural areas (namely Central Loire, Touraine, Anjou-Saumur and Pays Nantais), although local Vins de Pays and outlying vineyards also form part of the region. You can follow the river to find what they have to offer.

Key white-grape varieties

Chenin Blanc finds its greatest expression in the world in the Loire valley, where it is turned into dry, sweet and sparkling whites. In youth, its citrussy acidity dominates, but as it mellows with age it acquires lanolin richness and delectable flavours of loft apples, greengages and angelica. The finest wines, though, are the sweet ones, and when the

grapes have been attacked by the 'noble rot' fungus (see page 56) there's little to beat Chenin for taste or longevity – the magical apricot, pear, peach, honey, quince, barley sugar, marzipan and sour-cream flavours simply live on and on. The wines of Coteaux du Layon are the wines to try for this style.

Melon de Bourgogne is one of the most neutral grape varieties on the planet, yet it's responsible for the enormous volume of Muscadet churned out each year (after Bordeaux Rouge, Muscadet is the biggest single appellation-contrôlée wine in terms of production). The wines it makes, if you're lucky, are very dry, very light, very crisp and very clean, with a white-flower aroma, a thirst-quenching acidity and a pleasing iodine twang.

Sauvignon Blanc creates bone-dry whites, boasting the aroma of newly mown grass, nettles and flowering currant, and the tangy taste of white peaches, lime zest, redcurrants and crunchy gooseberries. The best wines of this style hail from the village of Sancerre.

Key red-grape varieties

Cabernet Franc is amazingly fresh when grown in the Loire and is the grape variety behind the region's star reds and rosés, such as Bourgueil, St-Nicolas-de-Bourgueil and Chinon. It gives perfumed, raw, just-picked raspberry-flavoured wines tinged with the smell and taste of blackcurrant leaves, all balanced by exactly the right amount of mouth-watering acidity.

Gamay produces juicy, peppery, squashed-strawberry flavoured rosés and reds made for drinking when they are young and fresh – and try chilling these for the ultimate experience. The wines of Cheverny are a great example of how this grape variety can perform here.

Pinot Noir offers dollops of strawberry and cherry flavours, though in a light-bodied kind of way. The village of Sancerre creates the best examples of Loire Pinot Noir.

Central Loire

A handful of wines are made in the upper reaches of the Loire, but they are produced in such minuscule quantities that all are consumed locally and, even then, they're usually served as house wine (they are not of shining quality, in other words). The serious winemaking begins at the ramparted, hilltop town of Sancerre and, literally just across the river, the flatter Pouilly-sur-Loire, famous for Pouilly-Fumé. Both offer benchmark Sauvignon Blanc for France, but the rest of the world has overtaken them for excitement. While Sancerre has the theoretical edge in terms of quality, in truth it's pretty hard to tell the two apart, though as the Fumé part of the Pouilly-Fumé name suggests, it's possible to detect a hint of coffee-bean smokiness about it (which comes from a special soil called silex, the French for flint).

A short detour takes you to the small village of Chavignol where you must try the historic and incomparable Crottin de Chavignol cheese made from curdled, salted goat's milk. You can eat it when it's freshly made, though the locals like to let it go a little mouldy before consuming it with, of course, Sancerre (a cracking combination as the acidity of the wine cuts through the saltiness of the cheese). Incidentally, the cheese takes its name from crot, the word for the small, terracotta oil lamp that was used to light the wine cellars before the advent of electricity. The shape of the mould that is used to prepare the cheese resembles a crot. Well, that's the polite explanation. Some suggest that the name derives from 'goats' droppings'.

Now here's a tip. If you like Sancerre, then you'll love the fragrant and snappy Sauvignon Blanc-based whites from the nearby villages of Reuilly, Quincy and Menetou-Salon. In fact, they're every bit as good as Sancerre, but distinctly cheaper.

Before arriving at the Touraine area, halt near the town of Blois and taste the wines of the Cheverny vineyards. In spite of plantings of good Chardonnay, Sauvignon Blanc and Chenin Blanc grape varieties, the best white – a delicate and searingly dry style – is made from the near-extinct Romorantin grape variety. The mainly Gamay-based reds are also fairly crisp and light-bodied yet still have flair.

Touraine

Before the river drifts by the city of Tours, it reaches Montlouis and, on the opposite bank of the river, Vouvray. While the wines of Montlouis and Vouvray are both made from the Chenin Blanc grape variety, the former is slightly less characterful. Vouvray varies enormously in quality and the cheapest bottles are disappointing at best and undrinkable at worst. Also, unless it's a sparkling version, there's often no way of knowing from the label whether you're buying a raspingly dry or a richly sweet style. Most are somewhere in the middle. But what a middle it can be – delicious honeysuckle aromas and mouthfuls of quince spiked with fresh lemon acidity. However, do not expect this from a cheap Vouvray – you won't get it. Always buy an individual producer's wine.

Talking of Vouvray, are you adventurous enough to try one of the traditional specialities of the area, andouillette cooked in Vouvray wine? This is a type of sausage made from spiced and seasoned pig's tripe wrapped in pig's bowel, which is then cooked in court bouillon and Vouvray for three hours at what is described as a 'quivering' temperature (simmered, in other words). Another, perhaps more appetizing, local dish, rillons de Tours, is also made from pork, this time turned into a sort of spiced, shredded-meat pâté, potted in its own grease. These peculiar recipes came about because, historically, each family would keep pigs (the most economic of animals as its entire carcass is edible). Only one or two would be slaughtered each year; consequently the local women became mistresses at the art of preserving the meat the pigs provided.

Moving on, the river now arrives at the source of the Loire valley's best reds: Bourgueil, St-Nicolas-de-Bourgueil and Chinon. Crafted from Cabernet Franc, these wines are complex and interesting, possessing the ability to age into meaty, almost leathery, raspberry-packed beasts sporting just a twist of attractive, earthy bitterness. A word of advice: always choose a single-estate wine as these are far better made.

Anjou-Saumur

As the Loire river floats in to this area, the first place to visit is the town of Saumur. Chenin Blanc is the grape variety employed for the generally dry, fresh and easy-drinking whites, while the reds, from Cabernet Franc, are pale and delicate yet very raspberryish. Some of the red-wine vineyards within the Saumur AC are entitled to the higher-quality appellation of Saumur-Champigny and this is another top-quality wine – silky soft yet full-bodied, with lashings of succulent raspberry and blackcurrant fruit, this is a real joy to drink.

Sparkling wine is what Saumur makes the most of (in terms of volume), though, thanks to cool ripening conditions and a chalky, limestone soil called tuffeau. This was the earth that was excavated to construct the famous châteaux along the river banks and the gaping holes left behind became the tunnels and cellars in which the fizz is matured, all 1000 km (625 miles) of them (spookily, the same length as the river itself). Produced in the same way as champagne, these are sharp, lively wines, bursting with appley fruit.

The river now meanders towards the Anjou district, but most of its wines deserve a wide berth because they're very plain and ordinary on the whole. The first exception is Savennières, a superb, 100 per cent Chenin Blanc, dry white wine that ages well, especially when the fruit hails from the tiny, top-notch, Grand Cru vineyards of Coulée-de-Serrant and la Roche-aux-Moines that lie on steep slopes rising from the riverside. The second is Cabernet d'Anjou, an off-dry, juicy-fruited rosé made from the Cabernet Franc grape variety. Finally, keep an eye on a wine labelled Anjou-Villages Brissac – this is an exciting new sub-appellation making juicy reds from Cabernet Franc and a little Cabernet Sauvignon. You might also check out Gamay d'Anjou from an individual producer. It can be rustic but tasty.

The perfect sweet, long-lived white Loire wine is found nearby in the hugely underrated Coteaux du Layon. Look in particular for the stunning Quarts-de-Chaume and the great value Bonnezeaux, both sharing intensely rich flavours of peach and honey (these are sub-zones of Coteaux du Layon that have their own appellations contrôlées).

197

Pays Nantais

The river's journey is now almost over as it glides unhurriedly past the granite vineyards of Pays Nantais, where Muscadet – the most famous ambassador of all Loire wines – is made. As dry as wine can be, this is the ideal partner to the seafood and freshwater fish dishes for which this area is famed – and don't miss the Breton oysters sprinkled with Muscadet, adored by the locals.

The very basic styles (simply labelled Muscadet) can often be lifeless and bland, so trade up to the more minerally Muscadet de Sèvre-et-Maine, the fuller-bodied Muscadet des Coteaux de la Loire or the softer Muscadet de Côtes de Grand-Lieu. Top wines bear 'sur lie' on their label, meaning that they are bottled straight from their lees – that yeasty sediment formed during fermentation – to emphasize character and to add a greater depth of creamy, nutty flavour and a burst of spritz.

Gros Plant du Pays Nantais is a notch down in quality from its Muscadet cousin – a sharp, searing, iodiney wine perfect for fruits de mer and not much else. And Vin de Pays des Marches de Bretagne (a red wine) is hardly something you'll find in the UK, but merits a swig if you ever find yourself near the river's mouth, as some can be fair enough. Also worth trying are Vin de Pays du Jardin de la France Sauvignon Blanc or Chardonnay, the up-and-coming, easy-drinking Haut-Poitou (red and white) and, last but not least, Crémant de Loire, a softer, creamier and higher-quality version of basic sparkling Loire.

WHEN TO DRINK LOIRE VALLEY WINES
▸ The simplest styles are intended for immediate drinking
▸ Mid-priced, dry whites will keep for between three and five years from the vintage date
▸ Quincy can last for two years
▸ Sancerre can age for five years plus
▸ Dry Vouvray is best after six to eight years
▸ Bourgueil, St-Nicolas-de-Bourgueil and Saumur-Champigny can age for six to ten years

▸ Savennières needs six to eight years before it is particularly enjoyable
▸ Bonnezeaux and Quarts-de-Chaume should to be cellared for at least ten years
▸ Coteaux du Layon is ready at 12 years, but lasts for ever
▸ Chinon can be drunk young yet can live for 20 years
▸ Top sweet Vouvray is worth keeping for 20 years at least

Food and wine matching

Loire reds and rosés are perfect for any kind of hot-weather barbecue fare (especially if you chill them right down) because they have enough complexity to stand up to the challenge that this kind of food so often presents (burnt bits, the fumes and flavours of charcoal and so on) without being too heavy and demanding.

Turning to the white wines, treat yourself to a single-estate Sancerre if you're eating lobster, though it's also a terrific complement to gazpacho, warm bacon and avocado salad, smoked trout, southern-fried chicken. Any dry white from the Loire will go well with any Indian or southeast Asian recipe thanks to their generous acidic bite, which counteracts the spiciness of Indian and Far Eastern cooking.

Muscadet, by its very neutral character, does more than just partner the local seafood and fish. You can drink it with virtually anything you want, including Caesar salad, carpaccio, hummus, spinach and ricotta lasagne, prosciutto, chicken Kiev, spaghetti carbonara, tomato and mozzarella salad, pizza, tuna pasta bake and sushi.

BEAUJOLAIS

Convention describes Beaujolais as the southernmost sub-region of Burgundy because together they form one of France's administrative regions. But if you were to divide French wines by the geological contours of the land, then Beaujolais would always be considered as an extension of the northern Rhône valley since they have been shaped by geological forces quite different to those of Burgundy. However, Beaujolais enjoys an identity of its own, bearing little resemblance to either Burgundy or northern Rhône.

For a start, the majestic, steep-sided gorges of the northern Rhône have given way to a picture-postcard landscape of rolling hills – the Monts du Beaujolais that run down from Mâcon to Lyon – studded with farms and pretty little villages. The weather is different, too. It's much warmer and sunnier than Burgundy, but Beaujolais doesn't have the extremes of summertime heat experienced by the Rhône region. And the sunshine brings with it a great joie de vivre in the people – you won't find here any of the austerity of its northern neighbour – and this sense of fun is also the hallmark of the region's wines.

While a tiny amount of Chardonnay and Aligoté grape varieties are grown, it is the Gamay grape variety that is king here, making the purple-coloured, light-bodied, easy-drinking red wines for which the region is so famous. While all exude glorious aromas and flavours of strawberry fruit gums, ripe bananas and juicy peaches, there are some differences in quality, depending on precisely where the grapes are grown.

The southern half of Beaujolais is where the bulk of the wine is created, which is simply labelled Beaujolais. Some 80 million bottles of this everyday quaffing style are produced each year and, of this, 40 per cent is sold as Beaujolais Nouveau (sometimes called Beaujolais Primeur). This is released on the third Thursday of November, when the wine is just a few months old. Each year, Beaujeu, the region's capital, comes alive on the preceding Wednesday evening as locals young and old gather to celebrate the new vintage. On the stroke of midnight, they enjoy their first taste of the new Beaujolais.

A little aside here. Beaujolais Nouveau is quite the best wine to use to make the local beetroot and Beaujolais soup – delicious eaten either hot or cold. If soup doesn't appeal, then perhaps the thought of frogs' legs will cheer you up because young Beaujolais is also perfect with these.

Wines labelled Beaujolais-Villages are the next step up in quality and these are slightly more complex. They are a blend of wine made in any of the 39 designated villages, all located in the northern half of the region where Gamay thrives best in the volcanic, granite soil.

The best Beaujolais wines are known as Crus Beaujolais – and there are ten of them, each bearing their own appellation contrôlée. These wines have earned their elevated status because the grapes are grown on steeper slopes that catch more of the sunshine and therefore they supposedly ripen to perfection. The style of each varies a bit, but frankly their similarities are more obvious than their differences. Unlike other Beaujolais, most are capable of ageing.

Furthest south is the village of Brouilly, and the largest of the Crus, giving soft, fruity, easy-drinking wines. The vineyards of Brouilly surround a small mountain called Mont Brouilly, where grapes for the Côte de Brouilly Cru are grown on higher slopes where the air is much cooler. Gamay performs really well here and the wines are deeper in colour and more powerful in character. Moving northwards, both Régnié and Chiroubles are light-bodied in style and are ready for drinking as soon as they are released. The village of Morgon is reached next and, once again, the finest wines are produced from grapes grown on steep, elevated slopes, this time on the Côte du Py. These age-worthy wines are considered to be quite masculine in personality, which is the complete opposite of one of the best-known Beaujolais Crus: the delightful, perfumed, sweet-fruited and feminine (but over-priced) Fleurie. Another well-known name, Moulin-à-Vent, is perhaps the finest wine of the region. This can also be tucked away for quite a few years, during which it takes on a chocolatey, almost Burgundian character. The journey ends at Chénas, Juliénas and St-Amour, at the top of the region where the sun doesn't shine quite so brightly. Here, the grapes ripen more slowly, giving wines of some intensity.

201

**WHEN TO DRINK
BEAUJOLAIS**
▶ Simple Beaujolais,
Beaujolais Nouveau,
Brouilly, Régnié and
Chiroubles should be
drunk when they are
young and fresh. Indeed,
almost all Beaujolais
can be drunk within a
year. But if you want to
experiment, Juliénas and
St-Amour repays keeping
for one to two years from
the vintage date
▶ Fleurie and Chénas is
also delicious young, but
most can be cellared for
two to three years
▶ Côte de Brouilly can age
for several years, but why
wait? Morgon and Moulin-
à-Vent do make some
styles that like ageing
and may improve for
five to six years, but
much Morgon can be
drunk young

The making of Beaujolais

The gluggable wines of Beaujolais are produced via a fermentation method known as carbonic maceration. This process is designed to emphasize freshness and fruitiness, and to minimize the extraction of tannin and acids from the skins of the grapes. So how does it work?

Whole bunches of uncrushed grapes are piled into stainless-steel fermentation vats that are then sealed. The weight of the grapes at the top of the vat causes the skins of the grapes at the bottom to burst and their juice starts to ferment in the normal way.

Heat is a by-product of fermentation and as the temperature inside the vat increases, the grapes at the top begin to ferment inside their skins. Because these grapes remain intact, the fermenting pulp cannot draw out the tannin and acids that the skins contain.

Carbon dioxide, which is also released during the normal fermentation process, rises to the top of the vat, and since it cannot escape, forms a protective blanket over the fermenting wine to create an anaerobic environment. In other words, oxygen is excluded completely, which helps to keep the new wine as fresh and fruity as wine can be.

Food and wine matching

Beaujolais is by far the best wine to drink with starters such as salami, pea and ham soup or hot chicken liver salad, thanks to its light-bodied style. For the same reason, it's also a perfect partner to gammon, moussaka, kleftiko – and even haggis. Choose a Beaujolais Cru, however, for cottage pie, calves' liver or grilled salmon (which proves the point that you can drink red wine with fish).

THE SOUTHWEST

The southwest corner of France is home to around 30 separate winemaking areas – and separate is the word to stress here because this is not a single, homogeneous wine region like Alsace, say. Instead, groups of vineyards are scattered across a diverse variety of landscapes stretching eastwards from the border of the Bordeaux region towards the city of Toulouse and southwards towards the Pyrénées. The only thing these vineyards have in common is the characterful wine they produce (often from unusual – and sometimes ancient – local grape varieties), some of them among the most underrated in France.

The Dordogne and the Bordeaux look-alikes

Where better to start a trip around the southwest than in the beautiful, rural valley of the Dordogne with its photogenic castles and forts, a legacy dating from the final battles of the Hundred Years War? The Dordogne is just a hop and a skip away from the Bordeaux region, so it's not surprising that the wines of the two areas taste very similar. For a start, the same blends of grape varieties are used, namely Cabernet Sauvignon, Cabernet Franc and Merlot for the reds and Sauvignon Blanc and Sémillon for the whites, and the soils and climate are virtually identical. The major difference is that wines made here are lighter in body, have a slightly grassier taste and don't age so well. Nevertheless, they are extremely interesting, highly drinkable and – the best bit of all – are sold at bargain prices.

Pleasant, everyday reds and whites are labelled Bergerac, Côtes de Bergerac and Montravel, but by far the best red of the valley is the delicious blackcurranty Pécharmant that the locals describe as 'tasting of the soil'. They consider Pécharmant just the right wine to drink with hefty winter dishes such as civet de lièvre (jugged hare) and lièvre à la Royale, a long-cooked concoction of hare slow-cooked in its own blood.

For slightly sweeter whites, look for Côtes de Montravel and Haut-Montravel, the latter being the sweeter of the two. Côtes de Bergerac Moelleux, Rosette and Saussignac are even sweeter. The finest sweet wine of the Dordogne, though, is Monbazillac, made from grapes grown on misty slopes running down to the river. The mist encourages 'noble rot' (see page 56), which is responsible for the delectable flavours that mark the top sweet white wines of France – a mouth-filling sweetness of peaches and pineapples in syrup, perfumed with ginger and apricot blossom. Indeed, these can be the sweetest wines of France. A word of warning, however: while Monbazillac can often compete with Bordeaux's top sweet wines for quality, it's best to choose wines from single properties only – merchant and co-operative labels won't be nearly so rich. To find out more about the wines of the Dordogne, explore any of the four wine routes that all start in the town of Bergerac.

Further south lie the wine areas of Côtes de Duras, Côtes du Marmandais, Buzet and Côtes du Brulhois, where, once again, the Bordeaux influence can be felt, although the Côtes du Marmandais and Côtes du Brulhois are also allowed to use grape varieties such as Syrah, Tannat, Fer Servadou and Cot (the local name for Malbec) in their red blends. Most of the wines are made by local co-operatives and they are generally easy-drinking wines of good value.

All of these Bordeaux look-alikes are perfect matches to the celebrated regional Périgord specialities of black truffles (often described as the 'black diamond') and foie gras (produced from both duck and Périgord geese). Indeed, when you see 'à la Périgourdine' on the menu, you can be certain that truffles and foie gras are going to form part of the ingredients of a sauce or stuffing. For example, ballottine de lièvre à la Périgourdine is hare stuffed with veal, rabbit or pork and foie gras and truffles, all flavoured with brandy (some dish), while cassoulet Périgourdine is a wholesome, slow-cooked stew of mutton, white haricot beans, garlic sausage and goose neck stuffed with truffles and foie gras. Looking at these ingredients, it seems hard to believe that this is supposed to be a peasant's dish. And having mentioned the word dish, cassoulet is named after the distinctive, oval-shape, covered earthenware pot in which it is cooked. It is traditional to deglaze the pot from the previous cassoulet to provide the base for the next one, which has led to legendary tales of a 'single' cassoulet lasting several decades.

Before leaving the Dordogne, make a point of visiting the market in either Beaulieu-sur-Dordogne or Meyssac to try Vin de Paille de Corrèze. Traditionally, this fascinating, ultra-sweet wine made from grapes that have been left to dry out on straw mats was served as an aperitif at every family celebration, but the habit faded for no known reason and the wine died out. A few entrepreneurial winemakers have revived it, however, and it's becoming very popular once again.

The Tarn valley

The talons of Bordeaux are left far behind as you journey eastwards up the Tarn river valley towards Toulouse – famous for its eponymous type of spicy sausage – to the Côtes du Frontonnais. The Négrette grape variety reigns here, languishing in the heat of sun-soaked slopes to give one of the most distinctive red wines in southwest France – scented with tobacco and pepper and filled with the velvety smooth flavours of juicy raspberries and strawberries, aniseed and liquorice. Most of this wine is drunk in Toulouse, which is a good enough reason in itself to visit this historic city.

Further up the Tarn lies the horseshoe of vineyards that makes up the area of Gaillac. There is much potential here if only someone would harness it, but, having said that, some 27 million bottles of Gaillac wines are produced each year, so somebody likes these wines already. A broad range of styles is produced, from dry to sweet, from white to red, from still to sparkling. The best, from the most conscientious producers, are the aromatic dry whites made from the Mauzac and Len de l'El grape varieties (the latter translating as 'out of sight') that result in white wines with a crisp green-apple flavour. The best wine of the district, however, is the trendy Gaillac Mousseux, a fizzy wine made either by the traditional method or the méthode rurale. This can be a fabulous mouthful of tropical orchard fruit, off dry in sweetness.

And now for something completely different

Northwest of Gaillac in the serpentine Lot valley, the village of Cahors produces one of France's most distinctive and unusual wines – one of which also happens to be one of the leading reds of the southwest. Here, the Auxerrois grape variety – yet another name for Malbec – thrives on a high, wild, arid, limestone plateau (known as a 'causse') to give gutsy, tannic, long-lasting wines with pronounced aromas and flavours of prunes, coffee and tobacco, occasionally a richness of damsons and, rather too often, an aftertaste of what can only be described as iron filings. Historically, Cahors was known as the black wine in the Russian market where it sold well during the nineteenth century thanks to its unusually deep colour, explained by the fact that the grapes used to be baked or boiled before they were fermented. The Russians' love affair with Cahors came about when Russian merchants took the wine home as a gift to the Orthodox church. They started to use it during Mass and soon the Russian tsars were drinking huge quantities of it. Believe it or not, it is given to the macaques at Lipetsk zoo in western Russia to help keep them warm during the winter freeze. But back to France. Nowadays, the wines remain dark, but are definitely not black. Indeed, some lighter styles are emerging. All you really need with Cahors is some local cheese and a hunk of bread – simple country fare, but, oh, so good.

While you are on the causse, it's worth detouring 16 km (10 miles) or so southwards from Cahors to the Quercy area to taste the very promising Coteaux du Quercy wines – and, perhaps, to visit the prehistoric cave of Pech-Merle, famous for its incredible Magdalenian cave paintings. Also make a point of looking for the local causse goats'-milk cheeses called Cabécous, of which there are numerous types, including the soft and nutty, slightly blue Cabécou de Rocamadour, and Picadou, which is Rocamadour wrapped in leaves and aged, resulting in a much stronger taste. Also try Bleu de Quercy, a firm, blue-veined, cows'-milk cheese with a strong taste and smell. And talking of blue cheeses, Roquefort, which comes from the southwest, is one of the finest blue cheeses in the world. Even the fungus that causes it to turn blue bears its name: *Penicillium roqueforti*. This is naturally present in the atmosphere of the caves first dug into the hillsides of the in the village of Roquefort in the Middle Ages. Roquefort is the only village where this creamy, salty cheese can be produced – and the cheese continues to be matured in these same caves even today.

A completely different trip will take you to the ancient province of Gascony, the most southwesterly region of the southwest, well towards the Spanish border in the Vic-Bilh foothills of the Pyrénées. Here you will find the rugged wine of Madiran, made mainly from the tough Tannat grape variety along with some Cabernet Sauvignon, Cabernet Franc and Fer Servadou. This red wine, one of the most powerful of all French wines, needs to be decanted and it's one of those wines that really ought to be drunk with hearty food, such as roast meats and casseroles.

The Vic-Bilh hills are also responsible for a very good, pear and apricot-tinged white wine called Pacherenc du Vic-Bilh, crafted mainly from the rare Arruffiac and Petit Courbu varieties. Just to the north, you can find pleasant, fruity whites, reds and rosés from the area of Côtes de St-Mont, made from the same grape varieties as Madiran and Pacherenc. There's also Tursan, which produces a red wine similar in taste to Madiran, plus a good, crisp white from the wonderfully named Baroque grape variety.

Climbing further up into the Pyrenean foothills lie the districts of Béarn and Béarn-Bellocq, where it's probably wise to ignore the somewhat lacklustre wines and concentrate instead on trying one of the most popular Béarnaise dishes – garbure, a soup so thick that it's more like a stew or casserole. It contains cabbage, beans, potatoes and pieces of pork, bacon, Bayonne ham or preserved goose and is usually served with toasted or fried bread. But what about Béarnaise sauce? Well, though this doesn't actually come from here, it was invented in Paris in honour of Henry IV who was born in Béarn.

Next, you could explore the neighbouring Jurançon area by driving along the wine route, a shortish, winding circuit through the hills. Far superior white wines are made here, created from a blend of Petit Manseng, Gros Manseng and Petit Courbu grape varieties, used on the whole to make refreshing, dry white wines labelled Jurançon Sec. When Petit Manseng vines are planted in amphitheatre style in sheltered spots

207

of the valley, however, it can become so hot that the grapes start to shrivel on the vine, concentrating their juice in the process. The honey-sweet wines this juice makes (labelled Jurançon Moelleux) are rich in flavours of nuts, apricot, quince, ginger and cinnamon, all balanced by an invigorating splash of lemon acidity. Such is the history of this delectable wine that it is said that a few drops of it were passed over the lips of Henry IV as soon as he was born.

It's time to clamber even higher up into the Pyrénées, into the Pays Basque, to taste the wines of Irouléguy, where Tannat grapes are blended with Cabernet Franc and Cabernet Sauvignon to create a very robust mountain red. The whites (made from the Petit Courbu and Manseng varieties) are better, but are a rarity.

By the way, the cuisine of the Pays Basque is very flavoursome, which suits to perfection the more rugged red wines of the southwest. Lashings of local garlic, peppers, onions, tomatoes and herbs are used widely in both meat and fish dishes. Regional specialities include Bayonne ham, which dates back to 1120. This is cured for at least nine months with salt from the banks of the river Adour and is eaten either raw in thin slices or is chopped up and cooked in garbure or in pipérade, a dish of eggs scrambled with peppers, garlic, tomatoes and, of course, the ham. Turning to fish dishes, ttoro is a soup made with herbs, bread, olive oil and the water left from cooking salt cod, and chipirons en su tinta – baby squid stewed in a fish stock flavoured by their own ink – feature widely on menus along the coast. Then there are a number of regional, centuries-old cheeses (though not literally, you understand) such as Ardi Gasna, which means 'sheep cheese' in the Basque language. Produced from unpasteurized milk in large wheels with crusted yellow rinds dusted with grey mould, this hard cheese is highly prized in France for its sweet flavour and sharp, nutty aftertaste. Many of these cheeses are typically served with black-cherry jam – a delicious match to sweet Jurançon, thanks to its nutty flavour that complements nutty cheeses and its honeyed sweetness that can stand up to the jam.

Travelling around southwest France, you can't help but notice the vast amount of Vins de Pays on sale, the majority of them white in colour. Just 20 years ago, these country wines would have been best avoided, but there has been a spectacular turnaround in quality since then, a rejuvenation exemplified by the top-performing Vin de Pays des Côtes

WHEN TO DRINK THE WINES OF THE SOUTHWEST
▸Red Bergerac, Côtes du Marmandais and Gaillac can be cellared for three to five years from the vintage date
▸Cahors and red Madiran should be tucked away for at least five years and maybe much longer
▸Jurançon, Monbazillac, Pécharmant and Saussignac can often last ten years

de Gascogne, which is sold by the bucket-load in UK supermarkets. This is made from any or all of Ugni Blanc, Colombard, Chardonnay, Sauvignon Blanc, Sémillon and Gros Manseng grape varieties, and while its taste depends on the mix of grapes used, it is invariably fresh, dry, fruity and easy-drinking in style. Other Vins de Pays to look out for include Vin de Pays de l'Ariège, Vin de Pays du Gers, Vin de Pays du Lot (most especially the reds made from the Malbec grape variety) and Vin de Pays du Tarn. Frankly, though, why drink these wines in France when they are so easy to buy back home? Don't waste a single opportunity to try the far more exciting and unusual wines that are created here in the southwest.

JURA

Nestled close to the French–Swiss border in the east of the country, Jura is a dramatic, sub-Alpine mountain region that produces some very distinctive – and very different – wines. Yes, you'll find good, dry Chardonnay from here, as well as tasty reds and rosés from the Pinot Noir grape variety, the best of these bearing the name of the Arbois appellation on the label. There's also the delicate yet elegant, fizzy Crémant de Jura, which in its white guise is made largely from Chardonnay. But its pink form is teased from a pale-red grape variety called Poulsard – and don't worry if you've never heard of this before. It isn't cultivated anywhere else in the world and it isn't planted very widely even in Jura because it's such a tricky grape to grow.

Poulsard isn't the only unusual feature of the Jura region. How about Trousseau, another obscure and difficult-to-grow grape variety? This is used to make sturdy red wines, which are not to everybody's liking, quite frankly. However, Poulsard is called into service along with Savagnin and Chardonnay to help create the more palate-friendly Vin de Paille, a very classy, tangy yet sweet dessert wine, bursting with the flavours of caramel, honey, prunes, preserved oranges and a touch of red fruit. Though much esteemed, it is quite hard to find, but when you do, try it with foie gras (as mentioned before, luscious sweet wines are the perfect partner to rich pâtés).

Last but by no means least, Jura is also home to the strongly flavoured Savagnin grape variety and this is where life becomes really interesting because not only does it go into the Vin de Paille blend but it's also solely responsible for the region's most prized wine, the unique, pungent, yellow-coloured, curry-scented and nutty-flavoured Vin Jaune. Again, this curious wine, which dates back to the fourteenth century, can be something of an acquired taste – indeed, it is definitely not for the faint-hearted, thanks to its piercing, sour acidity. This is especially true if you are drinking a newly bottled example because, ideally, you shouldn't go near this wine until it has been in bottle for at least ten years. So what to eat with it? With such a posse of challenging flavours, do as the locals do and serve it as an aperitif with Comté, a regional cows'-milk cheese (that also has its own appellation contrôlée), and a handful of walnuts. Somehow, the saltiness and nuttiness of the cheese works really well with the wine.

The making of Vin Jaune

Following fermentation, the new wine is pumped into old oak casks and is then left to age for at least six and a quarter years (local wine laws insist on that extra 'quarter' for some reason). During this time, the wine is attacked by a bacterium called *Mycoderma vini*, which slowly forms a film of yeast cells (known as 'voile' or 'flor') over its surface thus protecting it from the worst ravages of oxidation, as well as imparting their own special, weird flavour. The casks are never topped up, so the wine eventually evaporates by up to one-third, leaving behind a liquid of amazing concentration.

The making of Vin de Paille

Here, the hand-picked grapes, harvested bunch by bunch, are dried out on straw mats, or by hanging them from rafters, to increase their sugar content before they go to be pressed for fermentation in old wooden casks. The drying process takes about two months, though this is nothing compared with the three to four years it takes for the juice to ferment.

SAVOIE

Savoie is often lumped together with Jura, mainly for the reason that they are such close geographical neighbours. It's true that both regions nurture some decidedly individual, native grape varieties, but the personalities of the wines they create are poles apart.

Most Savoie wines are extremely pale in looks, extremely light in body and high in natural acidity, which has much to do with the grape varieties used to make them. Chasselas creates the lightest, most salty-fresh whites of the region, the best hailing from the districts of Marignan, Marin, Ripaille and Crépy that hug the southern shore of Lac Léman. More exciting are the whites made from the Jacquère grape variety (planted throughout the region), thanks to their tangy, grapefruit, lime and angelica flavours. The best come from the villages of Apremont and Abymes. There are also the Molette and Roussette (aka Altesse) grape varieties, blended together to create Seyssel Mousseux, a frothy, floral-scented fizz. The finest whites, though, are produced from the Roussanne grape variety (locally called Bergeron). These are far more extravagant, delivering rich mouthfuls of apricot, peach and quince, though they still enjoy an invigorating snap of citrus-fresh acidity. In fact, thanks to the soaring acidity of Savoie whites, they are the time-honoured accompaniments to rich cheesy dishes such as raclette and tartiflette (made from Reblochon cheese, potato and bacon or salt pork).

Moving on to the reds and rosés, the vast majority are made from Gamay, but there's also a smattering of Mondeuse to offer a darker, more full-bodied and chewier alternative, packed with the aroma of wood smoke and the flavours of ripe loganberries and plums. Fortunately, both styles make excellent partners to Beaufort, a local cheese similar to Gruyère, but without the holes.

Savoie's viticultural pattern of cultivation, with vineyards dotted about in valleys here and on foothills there (among the ski runs), means that the wines are generally sold under the regional appellation contrôlée of Vin de Savoie, though the top 15 villages may put their own name on the label as well.

CORSICA

This spectacular, mountainous island is graced with mild winters, high levels of rainfall (by Mediterranean standards, that is), cooling sea breezes to temper a blistering summertime heat and plentiful sunshine over a long growing season. These all combine to provide perfect conditions for the cultivation of grapes.

But forget all about the classic varieties here. While all the usual suspects (Chardonnay, Cabernet Sauvignon, Syrah, et al.) are grown for the generally unexciting Vin de Pays de l'Ile de Beauté and Vin de Pays Portes de Méditerranée, Corsica's vinous claim to fame is its three indigenous grape varieties – Niellucciu (red), Sciaccarellu (red) and Vermentinu (white). In the hands of a good winemaker, Niellucciu gives full-bodied, herby and tannic reds, best drunk with the local salamis made from goat and wild boar, while Sciaccarellu (which translates rather wonderfully as 'crunchy between the teeth') offers lighter, smoother, cherry-flavoured reds with distinct aromas of pepper and coffee, which work well with figatellu, a delicious type of pork sausage that is roasted over a wood fire. Vermentinu can produce fragrant and plump whites that taste of apples, apricots and almonds – the perfect aperitif with which to wind down at the end of a hot summer's day.

The vineyards themselves are all located near the coastline – north, south, east and west – on the lower mountain slopes and flat plains where the original farmers were more easily able to conquer the thorny native bush. There is one overall appellation for the island (Vin de Corse) and, within this, five sub-appellations: Calvi, Coteaux du Cap Corse, Figari, Porto Vecchio and Sartène. The best wines, however, come from Ajaccio (especially when made from the Sciaccarellu grape variety) and Patrimonio (made from the Niellucciu and Vermentinu grape varieties), which both have appellations contrôlées in their own right.

Over the past decade, the introduction of modern winemaking techniques has slowly transformed Corsican wines from the mediocre to the interesting. Watch out for these wines.

WHEN TO DRINK THE WINES OF JURA, SAVOIE AND CORSICA
▸ Dry wines of all colours and styles from Jura and Savoie, as well as Corsican whites and rosés, should be drunk while they are still young and fresh
▸ Corsican reds will keep for three to four years from the vintage date
▸ Jura's sweet Vin de Paille and Vin Jaune last for decades

THE SECRET VINEYARDS
OF PARIS

You may be surprised to learn that Paris has become home to no less than 150 different vineyards over the past few decades. Admittedly, they occupy only 11 ha (27 acres) of land in total (to put this into perspective, the world-famous Château Latour, just one property in the Bordeaux region, comprises 65 ha/161 acres), but there is an ever growing interest in the wines they create, however quirky and folkish they may appear to be on the surface.

In fact, Paris has a long history of viticulture, dating back to Roman times when the city was little more than one small village in a collection dotted throughout this part of the Seine river valley. Every community would grow vines and, as the city grew in size, their vineyards supplied the wine to its thirsty citizens. Come the eighteenth century, the region had no fewer than 20,000 ha (49,400 acres) of vines.

In the early twentieth century, however, the vineyards of Paris disappeared, thanks to that extremely destructive aphid called phylloxera, which kills vines by devouring their roots. They could have been replanted, but there was no particular drive to do so: by this point, the railways had made it very easy to bring into the capital superior wines from other regions of France.

So what brought about the revival of the Parisian vineyards? Well, leaping forward to 1933, a group of artists was given permission to recreate the historic Le Clos Montmartre vineyard that had been located on the steep hill of Montmartre, just a few minutes' walk from Sacré Coeur and the Moulin Rouge. In its time, this vineyard had been home to a Roman temple dedicated to Bacchus, the god of wine, and a twelfth-century Benedictine abbey making white wine that was sold within the city gates (Montmartre was outside the city limits back then). To say that the artists' knowledge of vine growing was limited is an understatement, however. Against all logic, the vineyard faces north (in the northern hemisphere, vineyards thrive best if they face south so that they can catch as much sunshine as possible). They were also completely unaware that it takes four years for a vine to bear its first usable fruit and yet they organized a Fête de la Vendange (a harvest festival) for the year in which the vines were first dug into the ground.

Today, this tiny vineyard boasts 2000 vines (mainly Gamay and Pinot Noir), produces 1000 bottles of wine each year and a hugely popular street party continues to be thrown on the first Saturday of October. The wine is sold for charity at auction during the following April, the bottles bearing labels painted by local artists.

Elsewhere in the city, you can find a vineyard just behind the Gare St-Lazare, but of far greater note is the beautiful Clos du Pas St-Maurice, situated in the elevated suburb of Suresnes. Here, Vin de Pays des Hauts de Seine is created from Chardonnay, Sauvignon Blanc and Sémillon, and these are considered the best wines of Paris. You can actually buy them at La Taverne Henri IV on the Pont Neuf (EU regulations prohibit the sale of other Parisian wines by conventional methods).

Finally, a real curio: the fire station at 28 rue Blanche has had its own vineyard since 1904, though maybe saying 'vineyard' here is something of an exaggeration because there are only six vines. Indeed, only 30 bottles of wine are produced each year and, in spite of the fact that the wines are deemed to be on the verge of the undrinkable, the labels are highly sought after by collectors. Pity, perhaps, that a Californian wine producer has already grabbed the brand name 'Firestation Red'.

There are of course more French vineyards of note and countless scenic and historic places to visit on your wine tour. If you are planning a long trip or want to know more about any of the places featured in the book or television series, the Appendix that follows will provide some useful tips.

APPENDIX

Getting there

Route planning
It has never been simpler – or cheaper – to get to France and you can fly direct to one of the wine-growing regions through many online airline companies. Bear in mind that a handful of French wine regions – most notably Burgundy – are not served by direct flights from the UK. If you choose to fly into France, you will need to hire a car in order to travel around the wine regions. While all of the major players have their own website, www.holidayautos.co.uk is a good source for comparing prices and making cheap bookings. If you are taking your own car, though, you can easily book Eurotunnel and ferry tickets online.

The www.autoroutes.fr site (French language only) is an incredibly useful resource for negotiating France's autoroute (motorway) system. It shows you all the turn-offs between points A and B on your journey, as well as telling you where the péages (toll booths) are sited and how much they'll cost – and calculates how much petrol you'll need to get there. If your French is rusty or non-existent, both www.rac.co.uk and www.theaa.com provide a basic route-planning service to French destinations. The classic road map to use is a Michelin one – but you can also find the same resources online at www.viamichelin.com. Both the Michelin site and www.mappy.fr (French language only) can help you to navigate from one precise address to another; they can also suggest alternative routes. If you are driving, please remember that the French police take drink-driving very seriously indeed and often stop drivers at random to breathalyze them. If you exceed the limit, the penalties are harsh.

Professional wine holidays
You may prefer to leave your wine trip in the hands of the professionals, so here is a round-up of the best companies offering wine tours in France:
▶ The Rolls-Royce of wine tourism is provided by Arblaster and Clarke. Their tours to Champagne, Bordeaux, Burgundy and further afield are led by the crème de la crème of Britain's wine writers.

Contact: tel 01730 893344; www.arblasterandclarke.com
▶ Liz Berry (Master of Wine) and her husband, Mike, run informal wine weekends based at the Auberge du Mas de la Fenière in Arles in Provence. The focus is on tastings rather than winery visits, but the line-up of wines is always impressive.
Contact: tel 0871 474 0635; http://wine.weekends.monsite.wanadoo.fr
▶ The Wine Nose run tours to Alsace, Savoie and the Rhône, as well as perennial favourites such as Burgundy and Bordeaux. Emphasis is placed on visiting smaller wineries ,where you can meet the winemakers themselves and taste alongside them.
Contact: tel 0845 075 1048; www.winenose.co.uk
▶ If you fancy doing Bordeaux in style, Gourmet Touring Holidays will provide you with a pre-programmed GPS system and a luxury car before sending you off on a tour of the region's top wineries and restaurants.
Contact: tel 00 33 (0) 6 32 80 04 74); www.gourmet-touring.com
▶ And if you're feeling energetic, Winetrails specializes in holidays that combine vineyard visits with hikes or cycle rides through some of the country's most beautiful landscapes. Destinations include the Loire valley and Roussillon's wild hill country.
Contact: tel 01306 712 111; www.winetrails.co.uk

Arranging your own itinerary
Visit www.franceguide.com for a range of details about ferry crossings to hotels and B & Bs listings. A new website (www.winetourisminfrance.com) covers the wine regions in detail. Here you'll find logistical information, such as suggested itineraries for wine routes, details of cellar-door opening hours, locations of wine museums and dates of vineyard concerts and wine auctions.

Main tourism offices

ALSACE:

CRT Alsace, 20a rue Berthe Molly, 68005 Colmar
tel: 00-33-(0)3-89-24-73-50
email: crt@tourisme-alsace.com
website: www.tourisme-alsace.com

ADT Haut-Rhin, Maison du Tourisme Haute-Alsace
1 rue Schlumberger, 68006 Colmar
tel: 00-33-(0)3-89-20-10-68
email: adtpromotion@tourisme68.com
website: www.tourisme68.com

BORDEAUX:

Bordeaux Tourisme
12 cours du XXX Juillet, 33080 Bordeaux
tel: 00-33-(0)5-56-00-66-00
email: otb@bordeaux-tourisme.com
website: www.bordeaux-tourisme.com

CDT Gironde
21 cours de l'Intendance, 33000 Bordeaux
tel: 00-33-(0)5-56-52-61-40
email: tousime@gironde.com
website: www.tourisme-gironde.fr

CHAMPAGNE:

OT de Reims
12 boulevard Général Leclerc
51100 Reims
tel: 00-33-(0)3-26-77-45-00
email: accueil@reims-tourisme.com
website: www.reims-tourisme.com

OT d'Epernay et sa Région
7 avenue de Champagne, 51201 Epernay
tel: 00-33-(0)3-26-53-33-00
email: tourism@ot-epernay.fr
website: www.ot-epernay.fr

CORSICA:

Agence du Tourisme de la Corse
17 boulevard du Roi Jérôme, 20181 Ajaccio
tel: 00-33-(0)4-95-51-77-77
email: info@visit-corsica.com
website. www.visit-corsica.com

LANGUEDOC-ROUSSILLON:

CRT Languedoc-Roussillon
20 rue de la République, 34960 Montpellier
tel: 00-33-(0)4-67-22-81-00
email: contact.crtlr@sunfrance.com
website: www.sunfrance.com

CDT Hérault
Maison du Tourisme, Avenue des Moulins
Cedex 4, 34184 Montpellier
tel: 00-33-(0)4-67-67-71-71
email: cdt@cdt-herault.fr
website: www.herault-tourisme.com

CDT Pyrénées Orientales
16 avenue des Palmiers, 66005 Perpignan
tel: 00-33-(0)4-68-51-52-53
email: cdt66@wanadoo.fr
website: www.cdt-66.com

LOIRE:

CDT Anjou
Place Kennedy, 49021 Angers
tel: 00-33-(0)2-41-23-51-51
email: infos@anjou-tourisme.com
website: www.anjou-tourisme.com

CRT Centre Val-de-Loire
37 avenue de Paris, 45000 Orleans
tel: 00-33-(0)2-38-79-95-28
email: crtcentre@visaloire.com
website: www.visaloire.com

CRT Pays de la Loire
2 rue de la Loire, 44204 Nantes
tel: 00-33-(0)2-40-48-24-20
email: infotourisme@crtpdl.com
website: www.enpaysdelaloire.com

CRT Poitou-Charentes
8 rue Riffault, 86002 Poitiers
Tel: 00-33-(0)5-49-50-10-50
email: crt@poitou-charentes-vacances.com
website: www.poitou-charentes-vacances.com

PROVENCE:

CDT Var
1 boulevard Foch, 83003 Draguignan
tel: 00-33-(0)4-94-50-55-50
email: secretariat-direction@cdtvar.com
website: www.tourismevar.com

CRT Provence-Alpes Côte-d'Azur
Les Docks, 10 place de la Joliette
13567 Marseille
tel: 00-33-(0)4-91-56-47-00
email: information@crt-paca.fr
website: www.decouverte-paca.fr

SOUTHWEST FRANCE:

CRT Aquitaine
Cité Mondiale, 23 parvis des Chartrons
33074 Bordeaux
tel: 00-33-(0)5-56-01-70-00
email: tourisme@tourisme-aquitaine.fr
website: www.tourisme-aquitaine.fr

Burgundy, Beaujolais, the Rhône and Savoie:
These four winemaking regions blur the
demarcation zones of various administrative
departments. From north to south, here are
the tourist offices covering the area.
CRT Bourgogne, BP 20623, 21006 Dijon Cedex
tel: 00-33-(0)3-80-28-02-80
email: documentation@crt-bourgogne.fr
website: www.bourgogne-tourisme.com
CDT Côte d'Or, BP 1601, 21035 Dijon Cedex
tel: 00-33-(0)3-80-63-69-49
email: documentation@cdt-cotedor.fr
website: www.cotedor-tourisme.com
CDT Saône-et-Loire – Bourgogne du Sud
Maison de la Saône-et-Loire
389 avenue de Lattre de Tassigny, 71000 Macon
tel: 00-33-(0)3-85-21-02-20
email: documentation@bourgognedusud.com
website: www.bourgogne-du-sud.com
Rhône-Alpes Tourisme
104 route de Paris, 69260 Charbonnières les Bains
tel: 00-33-(0)4-72-59-21-59
email: crt@rhonealpes-tourisme.com
website: www.rhonealpes-tourisme.com

Practical wine tips

Buying wine in France
In many places in France, you can buy wines direct
from the wineries and this can often offer you the
chance to buy things that may not be easy to find
at home (and to make some savings, too).

Life is much easier if you are driving, of course.
Beyond the size of your boot, there is no official limit
on the amount of wine you can bring home from

France as long as it is for your personal use. Having
said that, H.M. Customs & Excise officers are likely
to quiz you if you exceed the advisory guidelines of
90 litres of wine (not to exceed 60 litres of sparkling
wine) – and, for the record, 10 litres of spirits,
110 litres of beer and 20 litres of fortified wine.

A day trip to Calais
If you live close to the Channel ports of Dover
or Folkestone, you can save money on your wine
shopping by taking advantage of Le Shopping in
Calais. Once there, it is usually best to buy wine
from the 'comfort zones' of Sainsbury's, Tesco,
Oddbins and Majestic's Wine & Beer World (as
opposed to the French hypermarkets). Here, you
will find most of the wines you can buy back home,
but they will very often cost 50 per cent less
(with champagne offering the biggest savings).

Simple storage solutions
It is an astonishing fact that well over 90 per cent of
wine bought in the UK off-trade (the supermarkets,
high street shops and the like) is consumed within 24
hours of purchase. There are plenty of French wines,
however, that benefit from being tucked away for a
while (in some cases for many years – the top red
wines of Bordeaux, for example). Even non-vintage
champagne, which is ready to drink as soon as you
buy it, will taste better if you hang on to it for six
months or even longer. Having said that, it is
perfectly feasible that it could deteriorate if you don't
look after it properly – and this applies equally to
less expensive wines that you don't intend to open
within a few weeks of purchase. So where and how
should wine be stored?

► Find the coolest room in the house and squirrel
your wine away in cupboards, wardrobes or drawers.
Any form of insulation helps, such as cardboard,
wood, blankets, polystyrene and even kitchen foil.
A cubby under the stairs and disused fireplaces
are also often suitable.
► Don't fall into the tempting trap of keeping wine
in the garage, garden shed or roof space because
wine hates seasonal variations in temperature.
► In an ideal environment, the ambient temperature
should be around a steady 10°C. The precise degree,
however, is not as important as being aware that it
is frequent and sudden fluctuations in temperature
that wine doesn't like, which is why you shouldn't

The following note relates to flying home:

If flying home, glass bottles rarely survive a
journey in the hold and on the carousel unless you
pack them in a rigid suitcase with plenty of padding,
and the majority of airlines – most especially the
budget variety – are pretty strict about the weight
of hand luggage carried on board.

keep it in the kitchen over the long term (with apologies to those of you with modern designer kitchens that incorporate a wine rack as part of the fittings!).

▶ Just remember that the warmer the temperature, the faster the wine will age, so avoid storing wine near radiators, boilers, cookers, tumble dryers, hot water pipes and sunny windowsills.

▶ Wine also reacts badly to sunlight, so keep it in the dark – drape a blanket over the bottles, if necessary. It also prefers a slightly damp yet well-ventilated location, free from vibration and strong smells such as paint.

▶ Bottles with corks need to lie on their sides: the cork then stays moist and swollen, thus providing an airtight seal.

Laying down fine wine

If you are contemplating buying top-class wine for investment purposes and don't have a traditional cellar, then it's probably wise to arrange for specialist professional storage because these kind of wines really do need to be kept in tip-top condition. Many fine-wine merchants offer storage for a modest annual fee per case, including insurance cover. Details of these services can be found on the internet and in the classified-ads section of specialist wine magazines.

The right temperature

Any wine that isn't red in colour does taste more refreshing served cold, though bear in mind that subtle aromas and flavours are masked if the wine is over-chilled. So how cold is cold, exactly, and how do you cool them down quickly in emergencies? Though the textbook temperature is 7–10 °C (45–50 °F), an hour or so in the door of the fridge is usually about right for whites and rosés. Having said that, Sauvignons, for instance, should be drunk cooler than oaked Chardonnays – the more youthful and acidic the wine, the more chilling it can take. Sweet wines and sparkling wines can be a little cooler, say 4.5–7 °C (40–45 °F) – a couple of hours or more in the fridge is perfect. Incidentally, many light-bodied reds (such as Beaujolais) taste really appealing gently chilled.

To bring the temperature down quickly, plunge the bottle into a bucket filled with ice, water and a handful of salt for ten minutes. Alternatively, invest in a reusable, chiller sleeve that is kept in the freezer – flex it over the bottle and the wine will chill down within five minutes. Remember, too, that you can place the wine outdoors if the weather is cold enough.

Red wines should be served at room temperature to bring out their fruitiness, but now that most of us live in centrally heated houses, this is not what it used to be! Aim for a cooler 15 °C (60 °F), though don't let the wine become too cold because it will then taste harsh. During the summer, avoid leaving bottles in the full glare of the sun because the wine will become horribly stewed.

If a wine is too cold, the quickest and easiest way to warm it up is either to pour it into a glass, cupping it between your hands for a few minutes, or to immerse the bottle in a bucket of lukewarm – not hot – water. Don't place bottles onto or next to strong sources of heat because the wine will warm up unevenly and will taste flabby as a result.

Decanting: when, why and how

Very few people bother to decant wine these days, mostly because the vast majority of modern wines don't need to be decanted. The exceptions are mature reds – top clarets, for example – which have thrown a sediment and so the wine needs to be separated from this sludge.

The first rule of decanting is not to be frightened by the thought of doing it. All you need is a torch and a confident hand – and the job is made much easier if you stand the bottle upright for 24 hours beforehand in order to allow the sediment to settle.

The first obvious task is to remove the cork, but try not to disturb the sediment in doing so by keeping the bottle as upright as possible. Now direct the beam of the torch upwards underneath the neck of the bottle so that you can see through the glass and in one smooth, slow, continuous movement, gently pour the wine into the decanter. Stop when you see the sediment reaching the neck of the bottle. Don't panic if it all goes wrong: simply strain the wine through coffee filter paper or, preferably, muslin. The worst that can happen is that your drink is slightly cloudy; the taste probably won't be affected.

Decanting wine also helps to aerate it as it is being poured, especially red wine, helping to bring out all of its aromas and flavours. It follows, therefore, that you can put your decanter (or even a large jug) to excellent use for those big, rich, tannic reds that need some air to mellow them, even if they don't have a sediment.

Leftovers

An opened bottle of wine will remain reasonably fresh for two to three days if you keep it in the fridge – assuming it has the cork stuffed back into its neck. Alternatively, buy one of the gadgets that preserve wine by removing the air from the bottle (it is air that does the damage, after all). Also, after a party, pour any dregs left at the bottom of bottles into ice-cube trays and then freeze them. This will serve you well when it comes to those recipes that demand just a tiny amount of wine for a sauce or gravy. But do label them properly; there is nothing worse than a cube of frozen white wine in a gin and tonic!

Further reading

Oz Clarke's Bordeaux (Little Brown) provides a down-to-earth guide to this complex, prestigious wine region.

Stephen Brook's Bordeaux: People, Power and Politics (Mitchell Beazley) is a fascinating exploration of the Bordeaux wine trade in terms of on how the wines are produced, marketed and sold.

Andrew Jefford's The New France (Mitchell Beazley) is a lyrically written and beautifully photographed wine-lover's bible. There are sections on all of France's wine regions, plus detailed assessments of its top producers and their wines.

Informative text, imaginative itineraries and insider knowledge have made Michelin's Green Guides popular with visitors to France for many decades now. Its *Green Guide to the Wine Regions of France* (Michelin) brings its authoritative voice to bear on the country's wine regions.

Mitchell Beazley's *How to Find Great Wines Off the Beaten Track* series (Mitchell Beazley) currently covers *Bordeaux* (by Monty Waldin), *Burgundy* (by Patrick Matthews) and *South of France* (by Jonathan Healey), but there are plans to add other titles in the near future.

If you're looking to get to grips with the geography of France's wine regions, *Wine Atlas: Wines and Wine Regions of the World by Oz Clarke* (Little Brown), or *The World Atlas of Wine by Jancis Robinson and Hugh Johnson* (Mitchell Beazley) cover not only France but also the rest of the world in great depth.

Oz Clarke's New Essential Wine Book (Mitchell Beazley) does what it says on the tin, providing a general guide to the world's wine regions and its grape varieties.

The Sotheby's Wine Encyclopaedia by Tom Stevenson (Dorling Kindersley) is a great source of information – a must-have for anyone building a serious wine library.

Wine Behind the Label by Philip Williamson and David Moore (Williamson Moore Publishing) is arguably one of the most useful guides to the world's wines. The book covers key producers around the world and rates the current vintages of their wines.

Finally, if your trip is as much about the landscape as it is about the wine, then *The Most Beautiful Wine Villages of France by François Morel* (Mitchell Beazley), with its gorgeous photos, will only whet your appetite for stunning scenery and charming villages.

INDEX

ACKNOWLEDGEMENTS

Elaine Bedell at BBC TWO

Sebastian Payne and The Wine Society for their cooperation. Also Tesco, Oddbins, Marks and
Spencer, Sainsbury's and Waitrose, Bryony Wright of ProvenPR and Champagne Perrier-Jouët.

At RDF Television: Grant Mansfield, Nick Shearman, Mark Powell, Hattie Pugh, Lucy Davie
Andrea Boscan, Sam Shields, Kat Korba, Conrad Mewton, Natasha Hughes

At RDF Rights: Rachel Barke, Mark Lesbirel, Fiona McGarrity, Carly Spencer

At BBC Books: Stuart Cooper, Eleanor Maxfield and Viv Bowler

Fiona Lindsay, Luigi Bonomi, Annie Sweetbaum

Design by Smith & Gilmour

Photography by Mark Reed (apart from pages 6, 62, 90, 106, 134, 160, 186 by Kat Korba)